CW00722211

Making the case for play:

Building policies and strategies for school-aged children

Issy Cole-Hamilton and Tim Gill

NATIONAL
CHILDREN'S
BUREAU
Enterprises Ltd

Published by National Children's Bureau Enterprises Ltd, the trading
company for the National Children's Bureau.
Registered Charity number 258825.
8 Wakley Street, London EC1V 7QE.
Tel: 020 7843 6000

Funded by the Department for Culture, Media and Sport

© National Children's Bureau, 2002
Published 2002

ISBN 1 900990 33 4

British Library Cataloguing in Publication Data
A catalogue record for this book is available from the British Library

All rights reserved. No part of this publication may be reproduced, stored in
a retrieval system or transmitted in any form by any person without the
written permission of the publisher.

Designed and printed by Spider Web 020 7281 3033

Acknowledgements

The authors would like to thank the following people for their help, support and guidance in researching and writing this report:

Children's Play Council Executive Committee: Patrick Candler, Paul Ennals, Adrian Voce, Jackie Martin, Christine Andrews, Hilary Smith, Joanna Ryam, Jo Binmore, Alan Barber, John Morgan, Stuart Douglas, and staff team: Sabina Collier, Pennie Hedge, Jessica Lubbock, Mark Dunn.

New Policy Institute: Andrew Harrop, Cathy Street, Peter Kenway, Steve Macarthur.

National Children's Bureau: Bethany Rawles, Emma Moore.

Department for Culture, Media and Sport: Margaret Prythergch, Tiffany Denny, Debbie Lye, Caroline McClean.

And also: Sandra Melville, Haki Kapasi, Tanny Stobart, Lesley Campbell, Paul Bonel, Mark Howard, Dave Wainwright, Glenys Tolley, Jill Arbuckle, Wendy Haynes, Jane Harrision, Steve Chown, Debbie Garvey.

Contents

Contents

List of acronyms

AC	Audit Commission
APW	Association of Playworkers
BVPI	Best Value Performance Indicator
CIS	Children's Information Service
CPC	Children's Play Council
CPIS	Children's Play Information Service
CYPS	Children and Young People's Strategy
CYPU	Children and Young People's Unit
DCMS	Department for Culture, Media and Sport
DDA	Disability Discrimination Act (1995)
DEFRA	Department for the Environment, Food and Rural Affairs
DfES	Department for Education and Skills
DH	Department of Health
DRC	Disability Rights Commission
DTLR	Department for Transport, Local Government and the Regions
EYDCP	Early Years Development and Childcare Partnership
HMT	Her Majesty's Treasury
HO	Home Office
HSE	Health and Safety Executive
IDeA	Improvement and Development Agency
IFB	Intermediary Funding Body
KCN	Kids' Clubs Network
LEA	Local Education Authority
LGA	Local Government Association
LSC	Learning and Skills Council
LSP	Local Strategic Partnership

NAFW	National Assembly for Wales
NOF	New Opportunities Fund
NOS	National Occupational Standards
NPFA	National Playing Fields Association
NRU	Neighbourhood Renewal Unit
NVQ	National Vocational Qualification
NWDA	Northwest Development Agency
Ofsted	Office for Standards in Education
PBNI	Play Board Northern Ireland
PPG	Planning Policy Guidance Note
QA	Quality Assurance
QCA	Qualifications and Curriculum Authority
RDA	Regional Development Agency
SEN	Special Educational Needs
SPRITO	National Training Organisation for Sport, Recreation and Allied Occupations
SRB	Single Regeneration Budget
WFTC	Working Families Tax Credit

Executive summary

In the last few years there has been a surge of interest and activity in children's play in England. Money for local regeneration and from the New Opportunities Fund has been used to develop and promote local play provision for children and young people. At the same time a skilled and committed play sector has been developing a more strategic approach to planning and delivering good local play opportunities and central Government has shown an emerging commitment to more strategic planning in the future.

Despite this, good play opportunities for children of school age in England today are still frequently restricted both in their ability to play freely in their own time and while in formal childcare. This not only denies children one of their fundamental human rights, it also limits their ability to enjoy themselves and socialise with their friends, to be as physically active as they would like – especially outside – and to benefit from the excitement and challenge that play can offer them.

Providing children with good play opportunities is also good for their families and communities. If they know their children are safe and enjoying themselves, parents feel more confident about their own activities and in many cases are keen to work or train for employment. Other community members who know that children are playing and enjoying themselves, while not offending others, also benefit.

The context for the research and policy development programme (Section 1)

The Children's Play Council (CPC) research programme, undertaken between August 2000 and January 2002, included an analysis of the views of children and young people and their parents about their play and free-time needs; a systematic review of published research into the value of play in the lives and development of children; an exercise in mapping strategic development and provision of children's play opportunities; and a survey of play professionals' views on the current state of play in relation to government policy. The findings of these research projects were discussed in detail with play professionals who helped develop the recommendations in Section 3 of this report. The programme was funded by the Department for Culture, Media and Sport.

The research programme focused on children and young people from 5 to 16 years old and defined play as being 'freely chosen, personally directed and intrinsically motivated behaviour that actively engages the child'. A clear distinction is made in this report between play and childcare provision.

In the past a considerable amount of work has been published on the theories and philosophies about children's play. These have played a crucial role in the development of a clearly defined set of values and principles for playwork and for the development of child-centred objectives for play provision.

Children's play is rarely confined to one place and children play in their homes, with their carers, at school, in the streets and neighbourhoods near their homes and schools, in playgrounds and parks and in supervised play provision. Wherever they play, children's needs may differ depending on their age, gender, ability, ethnicity and home circumstances. Whoever, or wherever they are, a rich play environment offers children a wide range of new and familiar experiences.

Children's play opportunities are provided at local level and there are many structures and agencies through which this happens. Perhaps, of all the services available to children, the provision of play opportunities is the most complex in its structures. Because of this, the actions of many agencies and departments at local, regional and national level have an impact on children's play opportunities. Where local planning is put in the hands of local people, in some of the new regeneration initiatives, children's play has been benefiting. But without careful coordination and planning it is likely that many children will miss out on good play opportunities.

The commitment, at national level, to promote the involvement of children and young people in decisions that affect them, to tackle discrimination and social isolation and to maintain standards is good for children's play and it is to be welcomed.

At local level there are a number of strategies and initiatives which can support the development of children's play opportunities. However, engagement with these initiatives by the play sector, while being fairly successful and effective in some areas, is very limited in others. Despite this there is optimism among play professionals about the potential for the development of play in the near future.

The case for play (Sections 2.1 and 2.2)

To play is one of the fundamental children's rights, as stated in Article 31 of the UN Convention on the Rights of the Child. Play is what children and young people do, primarily to enjoy themselves, in their free time. Play is the time when they can choose what they will do, how they will do it and what they want to get out of it. It is the time when they meet and socialise with their friends, are physically or creatively active in relatively unconstrained ways and become involved in activities of their own choosing.

Playing is an important part of children's healthy development. Evidence suggests it supports their physical health, their emotional and mental development, their learning and their social development. Good play provision is of value not only to children themselves but also to their families and the local community.

In some circumstances play and playwork skills are also valuable therapeutic tools when working with children with specific needs.

Issues facing children's play provision in England (Section 2.3)

Despite the good practice uncovered during the two-year research programme, there are still many issues facing the universal provision of good play opportunities for all children in England. For example:

- Involvement of children in decisions which affect them, relating to their play needs, is far from universal.

- In many areas, play opportunities are restricted by parents' fears for their children's safety, children's own concerns about the state of their play spaces, and reduction in the number of play spaces available to them.

- At the same time, in some areas, free open access play provision has been replaced by childcare services where parents have to book and pay for their children's place. This has particularly affected children whose parents have low incomes.

- Children frequently seek and benefit from excitement and challenge in their play, but they are often denied this because providers are concerned about accidents and liability.

- The range of play opportunities available to children depends on where they live and the relative importance local government and agencies give to children's play. The independent mapping commissioned by CPC found wide variation in spending between authorities.

- Too often the differing needs of different groups of children are overlooked. Older children, children who are disabled or have specific needs, children from black and minority ethnic communities, children in families with low incomes, children in rural areas, and those in traveller and refugee families, often have fewer play opportunities than others.

- Strategic planning and support for children's play at local level is far from universal. CPC's mapping found that fewer than four in ten local authorities have play policies or strategies.

- Although much supervised play provision is inspected by Ofsted and unsupervised provision is subject to regular health and safety checks, the implementation of quality assurance schemes is relatively low, with only about one in three children's play settings employing quality assurance.

- Staffing issues are of major concern within the play sector, with wide variations in the way local providers support and develop their playwork workforce.

One of the most important difficulties facing the development of sustainable children's play opportunities is resources and funding. Even among the 16 authorities in the Children's Play Council West Midlands mapping exercise, one council was spending ten times as much per play area than another and over four times as much per child.

To support play, managers and local groups have to apply for money to many different funding bodies. Much of this money is either for capital expenditure only or for short-term projects. As a result, revenue expenditure, essential for the maintenance and sometimes staffing of children's play provision, is frequently not available. It is all too common for children's playgrounds and other play spaces that become damaged or unkempt to be closed down because they cannot be properly repaired and maintained. It is a major concern that in a few years time, many of the new and exciting innovative play projects currently being developed may be unsustainable, leaving children with raised expectations but nowhere to play.

While the CPC research programme has undertaken and identified a significant amount of research into children's play, it is also evident that more research into the costs and value of different types of play provision, and into the effects of different programmes, policies and Government actions on children's play opportunities would be of great value.

The future for children's play (Section 3)

Children want and need a good range of places to play

For children and young people to have and make use of the best possible play and free-time opportunities, they need to have places near their homes and schools where they can:

- enjoy themselves and play with or without supervision from adults;
- choose and take control of their own play activities;
- play by themselves or with others;
- experience varied and interesting environments;
- challenge and extend the limits of their physical, mental, emotional or creative abilities;
- feel safe from environmental and human dangers.

These places can be indoors or outside, may or may not be specifically designed for children's play and may be staffed or unstaffed. The essential elements are that there are a number of such places in any locality, that they are accessible and available to all children who might want to use them and that there is sufficient variety to ensure plenty of opportunities to attract and satisfy the play and free-time needs of children of different ages, abilities, cultures and interests and with different home and family circumstances.

Parents and other community members must allow and encourage children's play

Even where there are good play opportunities, children and young people can only enjoy them if their parents and carers allow them the freedom to play away from their homes and other members of the community allow them to share and use public space. Parents and carers need to be confident their children are enjoying themselves and will come to no serious harm. Other community members need to accept children and young people playing as an important part of a healthy vibrant community.

Local government, partnerships and voluntary sector agencies are the main providers of play opportunities

For the most part the provision of play opportunities falls to local agencies. In the past this has primarily been local government, including metropolitan and unitary authorities, district councils and town and parish councils, and the voluntary sector. More recently Early Years Development and Childcare Partnerships (EYDCPs) and local regeneration partnerships have had an increasing role in providing for children's play, and Local Strategic Partnerships (LSPs) will have a vital role.

The involvement of local agencies and partnerships is wider than provision and also includes strategic planning, resourcing, infrastructure development and support and the monitoring and maintenance of standards.

Central Government has a pivotal role in supporting and guiding local play providers

Central Government alone can ensure universal provision. By promoting and supporting the provision of local play opportunities it can tackle the variation in provision across England and ensure the needs of those children and young people currently missing out can be met. This will help to meet the UK's obligations under the UN Convention on the Rights of the Child, especially Article 31, the right to play, leisure, rest and culture.

With a strategic, cross-departmental approach and the development of a national strategy for children's play, the Government could protect and promote the provision of good play opportunities for all children today and in the future.

Central Government extends its influence to local provision through legislation, policy development, direction and guidance, national standards, resources and infrastructure support. Infrastructure support includes the development of a strong, well trained workforce, research and dissemination of good practice and support for national, independent agencies.

Coordination of these functions might be best achieved through the development of a national agency or unit within Government for children's play.

Recommendations for the support and development of children's play in England

In response to these findings, this report puts forward 56 recommendations for action, aimed at local, regional and national agencies from both statutory and voluntary sectors. They include seven key recommendations, highlighted in **bold type**, which underpin many of the others. These key recommendations emphasise the need for strategic direction and focus, coupled with resources, at national and local levels. All 56 recommendations can be implemented without radical new structures or changes in legislation. They should be read with the implicit understanding that the expressed needs and wishes of children and young people are fundamental to the planning and development of play opportunities.

Central Government

Strategic development

Government departments should work with the play sector to develop a National Strategy for Play, along the lines of the National Childcare Strategy, which identifies targets for local play provision based on an assessment of the needs and wishes of children and their communities. The Strategy should be linked to the Children and Young People's Unit (CYPU) Strategy and help fulfil its objectives for children's enjoyment.
(*Recommendation 37*, Section 3.5.1)

Existing coordination initiatives within the Government, involving Department for Culture, Media and Sport, Department for Education and Skills, Children and Young People's Unit, and the Early Years and Childcare Unit, should be supported and expanded to include representation from:

- the Department for Transport, Local Government and the Regions (DTLR) (sections responsible for local planning, housing development, social housing and open spaces);

- the Department of Health (Quality Protects Team), and when appropriate;
- the Home Office (Community Safety Team), Her Majesty's Treasury, the Youth Service, the Audit Commission, the Improvement and Development Agency and the Health Development Agency.

(*Recommendation 38*, Section 3.5.1)

This cross-cutting group should work closely with public and voluntary sector agencies to:

- agree and promote the values and principles under-pinning the Government's approach to children's play throughout their relevant work programmes;
- develop objectives and detailed strategic plans aimed at providing the guidance, support and resources required to support local provision of good play opportunities for school-aged children and young people;
- discuss ways in which it can support the development of a long-term funding strategy for children's play;
- agree a programme of research into the impact of the National Childcare Strategy and other relevant programmes on children's play provision.

(*Recommendation 39*, Section 3.5.1)

Resources

There should be an urgent and comprehensive review of national funding for children's play with a view to developing a long-term commitment and strategy for on-going funding for local authorities and agencies to develop and maintain local opportunities for children's play which ensure agreed outcomes for children.
(*Recommendation 50*, Section 3.5.4)

Detailed research should be undertaken into the potential costs of providing good play opportunities for all children and young people. (*Recommendation 51*, Section 3.5.4)

Infrastructure support

Leadership
Government should work with the play sector to establish and support a national agency or unit within Government to guide and develop the play sector in practice development, research, evaluation, policy development and information dissemination with a brief to include all types of play opportunities for children and young people. (*Recommendation 52*, Section 3.5.5)

Developing the workforce
Government should continue to fund and work closely with workforce development agencies such as SPRITO in the development and maintenance of training and qualifications for playworkers.
(*Recommendation 54*, Section 3.5.5)

Policy, research and information
Government should develop its support for play research and policy development in partnership with the Children's Play Policy Forum, the Children's Play Council and other agencies. (*Recommendation 55*, Section 3.5.5)

Government should develop its support for the Children's Play Information Service (CPIS).
(*Recommendation 56*, Section 3.5.5)

Research and evaluation
Children's involvement in decisions which affect their free-time play activities should become an integral part of any evaluation of the CYPU's 'Core Principles'.
(*Recommendation 5*, Section 3.1)

There should be systematic monitoring of the implem-entation of the National Daycare Standards in out-of-school childcare and play provision and their impact on children's play. (*Recommendation 45*, Section 3.5.3)

There should be monitoring of the impact of the expansion of childcare provision on the availability of free, open access play provision, especially in areas with high numbers of low income families.
(*Recommendation 46*, Section 3.5.3)

A thorough evaluation should be undertaken of quality assurance tools including, for example, *Aiming High, Quality in Play* and *The First Claim* and schemes currently being developed, once they have become better established. (*Recommendation 48*, Section 3.5.3)

Research should be undertaken to develop comprehensive spatial standards for children's outside play that are sufficiently flexible to meet local needs while ensuring adequate space for children and young people's play and free-time activities. (*Recommendation 49*, Section 3.5.3)

Direction and guidance

National Government should support the development of local play policies and strategies through strengthening its guidance to local authorities on play in cultural strategies, through the active promotion of *Play as Culture*, and monitor its impact on the local development of corporate play policies and strategies. (*Recommendation 14*, Section 3.4.1)

Government departments and agencies should review existing guidance and practice development documents with a view to assessing the impact they might have on children's play opportunities. (*Recommendation 41*, Section 3.5.2)

The implementation of the Disability Discrimination Act (DDA) 1995 in children's play and play provision should be monitored. (*Recommendation 43*, Section 3.5.2)

A Code of Practice for full implementation of the DDA in children's outdoor play space should be developed, as agreed by DTLR. (*Recommendation 44*, Section 3.5.2)

Local government, partnerships and other agencies

Strategic development

Every local authority should work with local partners to develop and promote a corporate play policy and strategy as described in *Play as Culture*.
(*Recommendation 12*, Section 3.4.1)

Where there is currently no play development officer, local authorities, partnerships and other local agencies should work with the local play sector to agree a process and timetable for the resourcing, remit and appointment of a post with this responsibility.
(*Recommendation 13*, Section 3.4.1)

Local authorities, partnerships and other local agency staff involved in community consultations should automatically include children and young people in any consultation process involving change. They should seek out children who might not automatically come forward to take part and they should ensure they have consulted with children from all age groups whose play opportunities might be affected by the proposed changes. (*Recommendation 1*, Section 3.1)

Play development strategies should be routinely grounded in comprehensive local play audits.
(*Recommendation 19*, Section 3.4.2)

Local officers should be given the appropriate support, time and money to undertake local play audits and access audits.
(*Recommendation 20*, Section 3.4.2)

Any play audit or analysis of need should specifically seek out and address the views of groups of children who make least use of existing opportunities and provision.
(*Recommendation 22*, Section 3.4.2)

Local authorities and agencies with an interest in play should work closely with community safety networks, parks departments, and highways and traffic departments to improve safety in open public and play spaces.
(*Recommendation 6*, Section 3.2)

Local planning, development and renewal agencies and partnerships should consider children's views about their play needs in any new or re-developments.
(*Recommendation 2*, Section 3.1)

'Children's Champions' should be nominated in each local authority at elected member level and in each LSP.
(*Recommendation 15*, Section 3.4.1)

Local Children and Young People's Strategies (CYPS) should address children's play and free-time opportunities.
(*Recommendation 16*, Section 3.4.1)

Infrastructure support

Information, advice and training about children's play should be offered to people providing formal childcare. (*Recommendation 33*, Section 3.4.3)

Local agencies should investigate what opportunities exist for supporting the development of play associations where they do not exist. (*Recommendation 34*, Section 3.4.3)

Resources

Those with an interest in play should work with budget holders and fundraisers to develop sustainable funding for the development and implementation of play policies and strategies. (*Recommendation 25*, Section 3.4.3)

Local government, partnerships and play organisations should develop a local framework for funding for children's play which has at its heart the long-term maintenance, development and sustainability of local play opportunities which meet the needs of all children and young people. (*Recommendation 26*, Section 3.4.3)

Provision

The provision of inclusive play opportunities should become the basis for the creation or redevelopment of all children's play provision. (*Recommendation 21*, Section 3.4.2)

Measures should be taken to improve the availability of places where children can play. Measures should include:

- creating and improving parks and open spaces so they are well lit, overlooked and feel safe;
- providing playgrounds and facilities which are age appropriate, offer challenging play opportunities, in easy-to-get-to overlooked locations, accessible to disabled children and well maintained;
- providing supervised, open access play provision, staffed by skilled playworkers, which offers a range of both indoor and outside play opportunities and activities;
- improving children's mobility by reducing traffic speed and flow in residential streets and other roads

used regularly by children, and by considering the introduction of home zones.
(*Recommendation 23*, Section 3.4.2)

Local play planners and providers should ensure their provision is inclusive by providing:

- race awareness training;
- inclusive play training for all staff, from volunteers to senior managers;
- training in compliance with the Disability Discrimination Act 1995.

(*Recommendation 24*, Section 3.4.2)

Community development initiatives aimed at capacity building should seek out and encourage the involvement of parents and carers interested in developing children's play opportunities. (*Recommendation 7*, Section 3.2)

Schools should work closely with pupils, playground staff and specialist organisations such as Learning Through Landscapes to develop their play/break times and outside spaces for children's play. (*Recommendation 4*, Section 3.1)

Parenting programmes should include information, advice and training about children's play.
(*Recommendation 8*, Section 3.2)

Monitoring standards

Local quality assurance systems should monitor the extent and impact of the involvement of children and young people in local planning, development and regeneration. (*Recommendation 3*, Section 3.1)

The impact on children's play opportunities of the implementation of guidance and monitoring tools promoted by central Government should be regularly evaluated. (*Recommendation 17*, Section 3.4.1)

Regional agencies

Learning and Skills Councils should fund and support the development and maintenance of a skilled playwork workforce working closely with regional play education and training networks. (*Recommendation 28*, Section 3.4.3)

Regional Development Agencies should work with regional play training and development organisations to support the development of a skilled, qualified workforce. (*Recommendation 30*, Section 3.4.3)

The play sector

Local authority members and members of Local Strategic Partnerships (LSPs) should be invited to meet children and young people, visit play provision (both good and poor quality) and learn more about the benefits of play provision. (*Recommendation 18*, Section 3.4.1)

Work being undertaken by SPRITO on training and qualifications for playwork should continue, ensuring that the agreed play values and principles continue to be at its core. (*Recommendation 27*, Section 3.4.3)

Information about the nature, importance and value of playwork should be shared and disseminated widely to parents, providers and policy makers at all levels. (*Recommendation 29*, Section 3.4.3)

The research by the Association of Playworkers (APW), into pay and conditions of service should be supported and the results disseminated widely when they are available. (*Recommendation 32*, Section 3.4.3)

Existing play associations and networks should promote their activities so that agencies in areas where no such networks exist can learn about their value and role. (*Recommendation 35*, Section 3.4.3)

Inter-sector developments

The government should work with the play sector and higher education sector to continue to research the evidence base and 'what works' in the provision of play opportunities. (*Recommendation 53*, Section 3.5.5)

The play sector, with local government representatives and national Government, should develop a programme to evaluate the implementation of existing standards in improving local play opportunities and how these impact on children's lives. (*Recommendation 36*, Section 3.4.4)

Government and the play sector should work closely together to develop outcome indicators as targets for the local development of play opportunities. (*Recommendation 40*, Section 3.5.2)

Development work should be undertaken on the use of outcome measures based on the seven play objectives defined in the play sector document *Best Play*. (*Recommendation 47*, Section 3.5.3)

The play sector should work with relevant Government departments to develop a programme of monitoring and evaluating the effects of guidance on children's play opportunities. (*Recommendation 42*, Section 3.5.2)

A programme of public information dissemination should be developed which informs the public of the value of play to children, families and communities. (*Recommendation 9*, Section 3.3)

Successful projects should be identified and promoted where intergenerational consultation groups and projects mediating between children and young people and older community members exist. (*Recommendation 10*, Section 3.3)

Links should be created with organisations representing the views and interests of older people and people from different community groups to develop common areas of work on promoting community harmony. (*Recommendation 11*, Section 3.3)

Information and basic training in play and playwork skills should be included in the training and education programmes for all staff working with children and young people on a regular basis or managing play provision, supervised or unsupervised. (*Recommendation 31*, Section 3.4.3)

Section 1: Setting the scene

1.1 Background

1.1.1 Introduction

Children's play is one of the most important aspects of their lives. This report, based on a two-year programme of research and policy development, describes the state of play for school-aged children in England and makes over 50 recommendations for the sustainable development of play opportunities.

The development and promotion of children's play at national level in England is primarily the responsibility of the Department for Culture, Media and Sport (DCMS). The actions of other departments including the Department for Transport, Local Government and the Regions (DTLR), the Department for Education and Skills (DfES) and the Department of Health (DH) also have a major impact on children's play opportunities. While the provision of play opportunities falls to local organisations, including local government, partnerships and voluntary sector organisations, central Government has the overarching responsibility for giving leadership, direction, guidance and funding.

In 1991 the UK Government ratified the UN Convention on the Rights of the Child, undertaking to implement the Articles of the Convention, including Article 31, the right for children to 'engage in play'. The main instrument for implementing the UN Convention in England has been the Children Act 1989. This has focused on service provision for children whose lives and opportunities are disadvantaged by their circumstances, but has not addressed the play and free-time needs of children and young people in general.

In recent years, increasing concern about the evident decline in children's opportunities to play, accompanied by growing recognition of the importance of play for children, families and communities, prompted DCMS to commission research and policy proposals which would lead to a more coordinated and sustained approach to the development and maintenance of children's play opportunities, especially for children of school age.

To this end, over the past two years, the Children's Play Council (CPC) has undertaken a programme of research and policy development about play and play provision for school-aged children in England.

This report outlines the main findings of the research programme and draws on these, other relevant publications and the experience and expertise of play professionals to develop a set of recommendations aimed at national and local government, policy and campaigning groups and play professionals. The research findings are published in full in the companion book to this report, *Making the case for play: Gathering the evidence* (Cole-Hamilton and others 2002).

The programme of research and policy development had three strategic objectives:

- To identify the potential for play initiatives to inform and support key government policies, in order to find out what could work and why, in relation to play.

- To identify the key building blocks (both service models and processes) of an efficient and effective 'play development strategy' (that is, a coordinated approach to enhancing children's play opportunities at local, regional or national level).

- To build consensus and understanding of policy issues, research findings and good practice within the play sector and in related fields.

To inform this work, CPC developed a programme of research which:

- reviewed the evidence base for the value of play in children's lives and in their healthy development;

- investigated the benefits of play provision to families and communities, as well as children;

- measured the extent to which an adequate range of play opportunities currently exists for all children;

- identified the role that children's play provision currently plays in supporting national and local government policy agendas;

- identified existing structures for developing and supporting play opportunities and provision.

1.1.2 Children's Play Council (CPC) research programme

Something good and fun

In summer 2001 CPC collected 108 reports of consultations with school-aged children and young people and parents about children's free-time activities. These reports came from Early Years Development and Childcare Partnership (EYDCP) audits, Best Value Reviews, Education Action Zones, Children's Fund applications and other local consultations. Common themes emerging from the consultations were analysed and reported. Most of the quotations from children in this report are taken from the analysis (Cole-Hamilton 2002a).

The state of play

In autumn 2000 the Children's Play Council received 200 completed questionnaires from readers of *Play Today*, a free, bi-monthly newspaper for professionals with an interest in

play and play provision for school-aged children. The questionnaire was aimed specifically at those managing, providing and supporting local play services and provision in England and asked for their views on the importance of play and links between play provision and other areas of local policy development (Cole-Hamilton 2002b).

The value of children's play and play provision

Throughout the summer and early autumn of 2001 the New Policy Institute, an independent research and policy development organisation, undertook a major review of the most recent literature on play and school-aged children. They also contacted relevant government departments, specialist play and leisure organisations, national charities, university departments and independent play consultants. The objectives of the review were to:

- assess the published data relating to the UK's progress in meeting Article 31(2) of the UN Convention on the Rights of the Child;

- create an up-to-date record of the evidence that exists to substantiate the arguments for play;

- establish an initial consensus on the benefits of play and the value of play provision;

- identify a small number of exemplar play projects that have been developed in line with the Government's current policy objectives (Street 2002).

The planning and location of play provision in England

This was also undertaken by the New Policy Institute. Play policy, development and provision in England were described, variation in the extent and nature of play services and provision were examined and the reasons behind this variability explored. This mapping exercise was in three parts:

- **The national picture** – an overview of the structures and written documents that local authorities have in place for developing play provision, based on information known to regional play experts.

- **The regional picture: the West Midlands** – a more detailed look at characteristics of the provision, structures and plans within the West Midlands

'Play is what I do when everyone else has stopped telling me what to do.'

(Quoted in Bath and North East Somerset's Play Policy)

region, based on a written questionnaire survey of local play managers.

- **Local authority case studies** – an in-depth study of the planning and provision of play in four local authorities, including analysis of needs and the distribution of provision at sub-local authority level. The findings were based on structured interviews with local play managers.

The main objective of the study was to collect and analyse data regarding the patterns of current provision and the policies and strategies that local authorities are following in making decisions about such provision (Harrop 2002).

1.1.3 Play policy seminars

During winter 2001–2002 CPC ran seven seminars attended by over 170 play professionals in different parts of England. Each group discussed the findings of the four research projects and, informed by these and their own experience, identified key issues for change and made recommendations for the development of children's play. The recommendations in this report are drawn from priorities and proposals identified in those seminars.

1.2 Children's play

1.2.1 Scope and definitions

Children

This report focuses on the play needs of children of statutory school-age in England, that is between 5 and 16 years of age. Addressing the play needs of younger children is also clearly important but the paucity of well researched information about play and children of school-age was the impetus for this research and policy development programme.

As children grow up, their play needs and wishes develop. In particular, as they grow more independent they want to spend more time away from their home and parents. This review has therefore attempted to look at the changing and developing play needs of children and young people of

different ages from 5 to 16 years old.

As well as being age-related, children's play needs may also be influenced by their family situation and circumstances; physical, sensory and learning abilities; ethnicity or culture; the type of area they live in and their individual interests and character. In this report we have attempted to investigate and address how these differing needs can be assessed and addressed.

Play

This review defines 'play' as freely chosen, personally directed and intrinsically motivated behaviour that actively engages the child. This definition is widely recognised and understood in the play sector (NPFA and others 2000). In lay terms it says that children are playing when they are doing what they want to do, in the way they want to and for their own reasons. Play may take place with or without other children and any adult involvement is at the invitation of the child or children.

Children and young people of all ages play. As they get older the words they use to describe their activities change and they tend to use terms which describe specific activities rather than the generic term 'play'. Throughout this report the term 'play' is used to include the free-time activities of children and young people from 5 to 16 years old.

Play is different from organised sport, groups, clubs and classes which are clearly defined by external rules and definitions. This report does not include these types of activities in the term 'play' as they are not typically personally directed and intrinsically motivated (although they may be freely chosen).

Play provision

The term 'play provision' is used to describe settings whose primary aim is that children should play there. Play provision can be staffed or unstaffed, equipped or not equipped, static or mobile, free or charging. In general, play provision can be seen as having open access where children can come and go as they please, and the staff's main responsibility is in ensuring that children have access

'Sometimes I like to make stuff, sometimes I like to play games, sometimes I like messing about, sometimes I don't like doing anything.' *

to a range of quality play opportunities rather than adopting the role of substitute parents required in childcare provision. Some play settings do however offer parents a childcare service alongside the open access play provision.

Childcare

The primary aim of childcare provision is to offer parents a place where their children are looked after while they are at work or unable to look after them themselves. While children obviously play in childcare provision, and carers need to have an understanding of the importance of children's play, the role of staff involved in childcare may be different from those involved in play provision. For example staff in childcare provision may make sure that children do their homework or go to organised activities at the request of parents. This would not be seen as a responsibility in play provision. In general, childcare provision is organised, booked and paid for by parents, and parents are clear that the children will be looked after at specified times and in specified ways.

1.2.2 Values, principles and objectives

Public play provision is underpinned by a growing body of work that sets out shared values, principles and objectives. The Children's Play Council's *Charter for Children's Play*, originally published in 1992 and revised in 1998 (CPC 1998), puts forward a widely-quoted framework and agenda for improving play opportunities. Alongside this, playworkers and others have developed a set of values and principles about children and play as part of the National Occupational Standards (see NPFA and others 2000). Finally the document *Best Play: What play provision should do for children* (NPFA and others 2000) saw the development of a set of seven child-centred objectives for play provision, embracing both processes and longer-term outcomes.

---

* This and all other unattributed quotes are from children and young people, taken from Cole-Hamilton 2002a.

All these documents emphasise that play is a natural, healthy activity, and that providing good play opportunities means ensuring choice, equality of opportunity, recognising children's abilities, respecting children's needs and wishes and allowing children space, time and understanding for play, including managed opportunities for children to explore risk. These three documents are summarised in Appendix 1, page 62.

1.2.3 Play theories and philosophies

Claims and arguments about the benefits of play to children are based on an extensive literature of play theories and philosophies, including some very recent work (Hughes 2001). These theories, though they differ in their emphasis, assumptions and detailed conclusions, share the view that through playing children develop their abilities, explore their creativity and learn about themselves, other people and the world around them. Theorists have drawn on ideas from biology, psychology, psychoanalysis and neurophysiology. Some of the main theoretical approaches are summarised in Appendix 2, page 64.

1.2.4 Children's play today

Where children play

Children play wherever they are. This might be indoors or out. Children play in their homes, at school, in childcare and play provision, and in the public and private places they visit with their friends or with adults. For many children the primary outside play spaces are the streets and other open spaces near their homes. For example a study in Hull in 1990 found that 52 per cent of children used the streets and pavements near their homes as their most regular play space (Armitage 1999). More recent studies have continued to identify local streets, parks and neighbourhoods as important places for children and young people's play and free-time activities (O'Brien and others 2000, Wheway and Millward 1997, Greenhalgh and Worpole 1995).

'My favourite game is skipping. I like the beach. I play down my street. I go to the woods.'

Public outside spaces have an important role in the everyday lives of a substantial number children and young people, especially as a place for meeting up with friends. As children get older their concerns about safety in outdoor spaces shift from concerns about bullying and violence to more concern about traffic (Matthews and Limb 2000).

In Matthews and Limb's study of over one thousand 9–16 year old children and young people in Northamptonshire, the main reason given for being out on the street was that there was nowhere else to go. For the less affluent, the street was the main social forum. Young people out on the street were not looking for trouble, as many adults suspect, and most accepted adult constraints on the places they could use and the time they should return home. But for many, homes were seen as adult spaces where children were denied privacy and where there were frequently disputes over use of space (Matthews and Limb 2000).

Also, in most areas, there is some form of open access, dedicated play provision, for example unsupervised play spaces such as playgrounds, cycling and skateboard tracks, youth shelters and kickabout areas and, in some areas, staffed open access play provision such as adventure playgrounds and play centres. Parks and other green spaces are often popular with adults taking young children out to play and as places for young people to spend time together relatively undisturbed (Children's Play Council 2002).

Children are also increasingly spending their time in commercial play provision and in out-of-school childcare. This is different from open access play provision because it usually involves parental choice and costs the family money. One survey suggests that four out of five children who attend after-school clubs do so because their parents are in employment, education or training (Smith, F 2000). Holiday playschemes tend to fulfil a similar role. In general, parents pay for their children to attend these clubs and those with low incomes are less likely to use them (Cole-Hamilton 2002a).

According to McKendrick and others (2000b), 'the growth of commercial playgrounds in the UK is adult-led and can be attributed to the conjunction of a number of discrete trends that rendered their development viable'. These include the proliferation of the service and leisure industries, the availability of land and buildings and the growing recognition of children as consumers. Parental concerns about children's safety in public spaces may also contribute to this.

However, in another analysis of this form of playspace, which can include a range of play environments, McKendrick and others (2000a) note that it is:

'overly simplistic to suggest that these new developments are testimony to the new-found consumer power of children. Children play a marginal role: in the production of these play environments; in contributing to parents' information field prior to decision-making, and in the decision-making process'.

It is this aspect of commercial play provision that goes against the definition of play as something chosen and directed by the child (Street 2002).

The play needs of different groups of children and young people

As children grow up their play needs alter. They tend to become more independent, playing further away from home, developing and changing their interests and activities. Girls and boys may have different ways of playing. Play can be affected by children's religious and cultural background. Children who are disabled or have specific needs may sometimes require support or encouragement to play with their peers. Children whose family circumstances affect their daily choices, such as traveller children, children in homeless families or children in refugee families, may require detailed consideration of their specific needs.

Children and young people need to be able to play in the ways most suited to their own nature, interests and abilities regardless of their background or circumstances.

Work from the play sector shows that all children need to be able to choose from a range of play places and provision which offer them:

- varied and interesting physical environments;
- physically challenging environments;
- access to natural elements – earth, water, fire, air;
- places for movement including running, jumping, rolling, climbing, balancing;
- places where they can manipulate natural and fabricated materials;
- experiences which stimulate their senses;
- places to experience change in the natural and built environment;
- opportunities for social interactions;
- opportunities to play with their identity;
- environments where they can experience a whole range of emotions.

(Adapted from NPFA and others 2000. See also Hughes 1996.)

Mechanisms for providing play opportunities

Structures and mechanisms for delivering play opportunities vary from place to place as the result of a complex web of factors, which differ in each locality. According to play professionals, the main influences on the way play provision has developed in the past have been the amount of resources available, adult perceptions of children's needs, local government agendas, history and parents' needs. Children's expressed wishes have not, historically, been seen as important (Cole-Hamilton 2002b).

Even among the four authorities studied in CPC's case study research, the mechanisms for delivery of play and childcare provision differed. For example:

- **Responsibility for delivery** – neither of the district councils had control of the majority of local play areas (parishes had responsibility in one, while over half were managed by a social landlord in the other). In one of the urban unitary authorities the delivery of council-funded supervised provision was devolved to independent local bodies. In the two districts responsibility lay within a single service, while in the other urban unitary authority different sorts of provision were delivered by different parts of the council.

- **Non-council provision** – all four areas had independent supervised provision receiving New Opportunities Fund (NOF) and Early Years Development and Childcare (EYDCP) support (although in a more rural district they were very few in number) and more traditional youth clubs. Schools or school-based community organisations were key deliverers in all four case study areas. Other partners included community organisations, commercial daycare providers, parish councils, a national charity, and a county playing field association.

- **Term-time clubs** – all the authorities funded term-time provision, although there was considerable variation in their quantity and style, with some being orientated towards sport, art, study support or childcare. In one of the district councils the clubs had a development remit, running only while the council helps independent provision launch in their place.

- **Holiday play schemes** – there were local authority, funded summer playschemes as well as independent projects in all four case study areas. There seemed to be little variation in approach to this, with an overlap between play and more organised activities, such as sport and art.

- **Other provision** – apart from provision for children with specific needs, there were several examples of other types of provision from the case studies: one urban unitary authority had two council-funded open-access play centres and one rural district council had a voluntary sector play bus and children's farm.

One district council had transformed itself from a traditional play service into a development agency that is delivering supervised provision until it is able to get an independent successor up and running as a replacement (Harrop 2002).

'We play around the dustbins –
we hide behind them and jump
on the lids.'

1.3 Children's play and the current policy agenda

1.3.1 National social and economic policy

The main aims of the current government's social and economic policy agenda, as it affects children and young people, are to reduce child poverty, reduce social exclusion, reduce crime, increase children's involvement in decisions that affect them and increase educational achievement.

The proposed strategy for children and young people

The proposed government framework for developing services that support and enhance opportunities for children and young people states that all children and young people should be assured, among other things, of:

- real opportunities to fulfil their potential and contribute to a fast moving, changing and interdependent world;
- opportunities to experience the benefits of living in a diverse multicultural society;
- the prospect of living in a safe and secure community;
- chances to contribute to their local communities;
- the opportunity to appreciate the environment and develop a range of free-time and leisure interests;
- excellent, joined-up public services which strive to meet the needs of children and their families.

In addition, the Children and Young People's Unit (CYPU) framework identifies opportunities for children to play as an important part of their lives and development. The consultation document proposes that services for children and young people are evaluated on the outcomes they achieve for children and young people. For example, as part of the outcome relating to 'health and well-being' the CYPU suggest that children and young people should have the 'resilience, capacity and emotional well-being that allows them to play, learn, relate to other people, and resolve problems in life'. When defining an outcome measure to evaluate services aimed at promoting children and young people's 'achievement and enjoyment', the Unit proposes that the range of outcomes might include 'engagement in the arts, music, sport and wider leisure activities, access to popular play and leisure facilities; engagement in community and voluntary activities; a sense of achievement and self esteem' (CYPU 2001a).

Ensuring that children have a choice of good play opportunities available to them is, therefore, an important element in achieving these overall goals. Play provision and services are seen as having a positive impact on children's social, physical and mental health, their safety and their general inclusion in society. Over 90 per cent of the respondents in the CPC survey of play professionals perceived their play provision or service to have an important role in supporting these aspirations for children and young people. Crime prevention and community safety were also seen as important spin-offs of play provision. Play provision specifically designed as a resource to enable parents to work and train was also seen as important to families, to help increase their income and to the economy of local communities (Cole-Hamilton 2002b).

'Play is what happens when human children are propelled by a desire to know and understand, or by the thrill of attempting to transcend their previous limits ... it is, on the whole, what children do, and historically what children do has tended not be particularly important to adults, as long as they do it quietly and preferably somewhere else.' **(Hughes 2001)**

Involving children and young people

Current guidelines direct Government departments and agencies to increase the involvement and participation of children and young people in decisions and services which affect them (CYPU 2001b). Children's involvement in the development of their own play activities is fundamental. When there are no adults present, children will create and make their own choices. When adults are present or involved in planning children's play opportunities, they are increasingly soliciting the views of children and young people about what choices, resources and facilities should be available to them.

Tackling discrimination

Government policy is also aimed at reducing discrimination against groups of children and young people who have been excluded from mainstream services in the past. This includes disabled children and young people, who have always had few opportunities for free play or for playing with their non-disabled peers. The Disability Discrimination Act (1995) makes it illegal for service providers to discriminate against disabled people by refusing a service or offering a lower standard service, whether the service is provided free or is charged for. This means that those who provide, for example, indoor and outside adventure playgrounds and play centres, leisure centres and play areas in public parks, have to make reasonable adjustment to policies, practices and procedures that discriminate against disabled children. They should also provide auxiliary aids and services to enable or make it easier for disabled children to use the services, and make their services available by reasonable alternative methods where a physical feature is a barrier. By 2004 these service providers will be expected to make permanent physical alterations to their provision if these are required to make their service fully accessible (Scott 2000).

Maintaining standards

National Government also has an important role in developing direction, guidance and standards for local planning and service provision. Aimed at local authorities,

partnerships and other local agencies, these central functions can have a major impact on children's play opportunities (see Table 1.1).

Different mechanisms exist for promoting, monitoring and maintaining standards of local service provision and, although the some of these might alter in the light of the Government's White Paper *Strong Local Leadership – Quality Public Services* (DTLR 2002), a number have implications for children's play opportunities. These include:

- National Daycare Standards which require childcare provision to meet children's play needs and form the framework for inspection of all out-of-school provision used by children under eight years old (DfES and Ofsted).

- Best Value Performance Indicators which include the requirement to plan for play in local cultural strategies and a proposed local performance indicator on the development of play policies and strategies (Audit Commission and DTLR).

- Quality of Life indicators for sustainable development being developed by the Audit Commission and the Improvement and Development Agency (IDeA).

- Quality Protects objectives for play and leisure services for children and young people defined as being 'at risk' of disadvantage (Department of Health).

Government departments deliver a considerable amount of other guidance that can also have a major impact on children's play. This includes, for example:

- Guidance on Cultural Strategy development published by DCMS and now an accompanying guidance document on developing play policies and strategies prepared by PLAYLINK for the Children's Play Policy Forum and funded by DCMS (PLAYLINK 2002).

- Guidance from DfEE (now DfES) to EYDCPs and childcare providers on the implementation of the National Childcare Strategy, including *Promoting Play in Out-of School Childcare* (DfEE 2001).

- Guidance from DTLR to local authorities and Local Strategic Partnerships on the development of community strategies which draw together other local plans and strategies.

- Planning Policy Guidance Notes to local planners and developers from DTLR, on housing (PPG 3) and public open spaces (PPG 17).

- Guidance on the street design (Design Bulletin 32) and support for the development of home zones from DTLR.

- Guidance on community safety from the Home Office and Neighbourhood Renewal Unit at DTLR, including information and support to the Neighbourhood Wardens scheme and specific financial support to initiatives with children and young people aimed at reducing crime levels.

- Guidance and Codes of Practice on the implementation of legislation to promote the rights and needs of children and young people who are disabled or have specific needs in schools.

1.3.2 Local planning, regeneration and service provision

The provision of a good choice of attractive, satisfying supervised and unsupervised, indoor and outside play opportunities benefits from the active involvement of different local government departments, partnerships and voluntary sector organisations. Children's play should be an integral part of many local planning and development agendas (see Table 1.1).

In some areas ad hoc, uncoordinated provision may meet the play needs of many children and young people. But it is more likely that the needs of all children, including those with little access to a good range of inclusive play opportunities now, will only be fully met if all these agencies work together at local level and develop strategic plans for children's play, grounded in corporate, inter-agency play policies (PLAYLINK 2002).

Evidence from the CPC research programme indicates that, in many areas, there is some, albeit limited, liaison between those involved in play provision and local planning and service provision. For example, over three-quarters of the respondents in the CPC survey of play professionals said their service or provision was linked to at least one national or local government policy initiative, the most likely being the Early Years Development and Childcare Partnership (EYDCP). One in eight play services had links with four or more initiatives (Cole-Hamilton 2002b). Manchester offers some interesting examples (see Case study 1).

In the majority of areas there was some recognition of play services and provision in local authority plans. Almost half the play services were referred to in the Early Years Development and Childcare Plan and one in four in the Children's Services Plan.

CPC's West Midlands mapping exercise indicated that, although not clear-cut, strategic planning for play provision was more likely to occur in unitary, urban councils than rural and semi-rural councils, although some of the latter did have employees and planning processes for play. These were usually based in leisure departments. The research indicated that there was a good 'base' of activity in all parts of England from which to build, if policy makers wish to encourage more councils to develop strategic structures for the delivery of play (Harrop 2002).

Among the four local authorities investigated in the case study research, the main focus was on service-level planning, with little ongoing coordination between departments. Joint planning took place in response to external pressures (for example New Opportunities Fund funding bids) and organisations outside the local authorities had little involvement in planning processes. In recent years the two district councils studied had both implemented plan-based changes in the pattern of their provision, while there had been few major shifts in the urban areas. All the four case study authorities were in the process of a new phase of strategy development. Only in one was this specifically focused on play (elsewhere the focus was on cultural strategy development or Children's Fund bid preparation) (Harrop 2002).

Table 1.1: Local and national agencies that have an impact on children's play opportunities

Children's play place	Local responsibility	National responsibility
The streets near children's homes	Traffic and highways: traffic calming, street furniture, home zones	DTLR: guidance (Design Bulletin 32), resources, research
	Social housing: providing suitable play spaces, safety	DTLR: guidance and direction
	New housing development: planning permission ensuring adequate play space	DTLR: guidance and direction (PPG 3)
	Community safety: safer streets and public places	Home Office: guidance, resources and research
Parks, playgrounds and other public green spaces	Neighbourhood renewal: consulting, planning, providing and resourcing Parks, leisure, play departments: development, suitability, maintenance, safety, location	DTLR Neighbourhood Renewal Unit: advice, guidance, resources, research DTLR: guidance (PPG 17) DCMS: guidance on Cultural Strategies Department for the Environment, Food and Rural Affairs (DEFRA): 'Working for the Essentials of Life'
	Parish & town councils: development, suitability, maintenance, safety, location	DTLR: guidance (PPG 17) DCMS guidance on cultural strategies DEFRA: guidance on town and parish plans
Staffed, open-access play provision	Leisure, play, community development, voluntary sector: planning, resourcing, developing, providing, maintaining standards	DCMS: cultural strategy guidance DfES: setting standards (Daycare Standards), advice and guidance Ofsted: regulation and inspection
Formal childcare	EYDCP: developing, resourcing, providing, maintaining standards	DfES: setting standards (Daycare Standards), advice and guidance Ofsted: regulation and inspection
School	Schools, LEAs: policy, provision	DfES: guidance and advice, resources, research
Play for all children	All the above and social services departments: anti-discriminatory provision and implementation of Quality Protects objectives on children's' play and leisure opportunities	DRC: guidance and monitoring implementation of DDA 1995 DH: Quality Protects guidance and monitoring

CASE STUDY 1 Manchester – Adventure Playgrounds are integral to urban regeneration

Of the six Single Regeneration Budget (SRB) areas in Manchester, four have included adventure playground developments, or aim to do so.

One of these areas is Wythenshawe which, while being an area of major unemployment, unmodernised housing, poor health, relatively high crime and low educational attainment, has several major initiatives under way to create a renewed vibrant and prosperous area of the city. The development of Benchill Adventure Playground contributed to these initiatives. It is being redeveloped as its current location is on the route of the new metro service and it has to be re-located onto the site of a former school. It is being totally redeveloped at a cost of over £1 million.

A feasibility study for the redevelopment was funded by the Wythenshawe Partnership and the Northwest Development Agency (NWDA). The cost was £20,000 and it took 7–8 months to complete. The partnership was multi-agency and brought together public, private, voluntary and community sector organisations. Manchester City Council was the lead body in the partnership.

The study itself was managed by Manchester Adventure Play (a charitable company funded predominately by Manchester City Council), and assisted by a small steering group comprising representatives of Benchill Adventure Playground, Wythenshawe Partnership, Northwest Development Agency, Manchester Youth Service, Early Years and Play Division and the City Planning Division.

1.3.3 The changing face of play provision

Over the past few years there has been a major change in the approach to services and provision for children and young people and this appears to be affecting children's play as much as any other service. Much of the change affecting children's play is being fuelled by government initiatives and funding programmes including the National Childcare Strategy, Best Value, the New Opportunities Fund, the Neighbourhood Renewal programme and alterations in local government structures and funding mechanisms (see Appendix 3, page 66).

Play professionals are more likely than others to have an understanding of the potential for change in play opportunities, so in order to identify the potential for change in play services and provision, play professionals in the CPC survey were asked whether they expected any significant changes to the way play services would be provided in their locality in the next few years. Overall the responses showed that a small majority expected improvements. Some 55 per cent of the respondents

anticipated changes, 23 per cent were not sure and 22 per cent felt little would alter (Cole-Hamilton 2002b).

Of the 106 people describing likely changes, 43 felt that play provision would improve. This included 22 who anticipated an increase in play provision and 19 who thought play would have a higher profile in local planning and development. Two respondents thought there would be better coordination of the play service.

However, 12 respondents thought that local play services would suffer from lack of funding, and 9 thought that the emphasis on childcare and education was taking resources from play provision. Three respondents felt that difficulties with insurance and perceived risks to children would have a negative impact on their provision.

One in three of those anticipating change did not specify if the changes would be good or bad but were clear that Best Value Reviews, the Government's childcare and education policies and the 'social inclusion' agenda would have a marked impact on local play services and provision (Cole-Hamilton 2002b).

Section 2: The case for play

'States parties recognise the right of the child to rest and leisure, to engage in play and recreational activities appropriate to the age of the child and to participate freely in cultural life and the arts.'

(United Nations Convention on the Rights of the Child, Article 31)

2.1 To play is every child's right

To play is the right of every child. The UN Convention on the Rights of the Child, ratified by the UK Government in 1991, confers on children the right to play (Article 31) and Article 2.1 confirms that this right applies to 'all children ... without discrimination of any kind'.

While playing children also have rights. They have the right to be consulted on matters which affect them (Article 12), to express their views (Article 13), to meet with others (Article 15), to be protected from harm and abuse (Article 19), to services developed in their 'best interests' (Article 3.1) and to provision of an agreed standard (Article 3.3). In addition, disabled children have the right to support which promotes their active participation in the community and their fullest possible social integration (Articles 23.1 and 23.3) and children from minority communities have the right to enjoy their own culture, and to practice their own religion and language (Article 30).

Drawing together analysis of the implications of the UN Convention, Street (2002) highlights three main areas which need to be addressed in terms of a child's right to play:

- The provision of space: 'space is a basic resource that children need in order to play. It is by this measure that we can begin to judge how seriously a community is attending to the needs of its children' (Guddemi and Jambor 1992).

- Consultation with young people: is an explicit requirement underpinning the UN Convention, but in order for this to happen, children and young people need help in making their views known, and structures need to be put in place to promote their participation in planning processes (Adams and Ingham 1998).

- Integration of all children: in particular, those with disabilities is highlighted by Guddemi and Jambor – 'play is the right of all children' – which thus requires the provision of play settings which provide 'comfortable and equitable opportunities for integration of children with and without disabilities'.

In all three areas Street finds that there are shortcomings in the UK's implementation of the UN Convention.

'I like running around and stuff and also love making frogs. They make you think and I am pleased when I finish them.'

2.2 Children enjoy and benefit from play

2.2.1 Play is what children choose to do in their free time

Play and free-time activities are important to children. They are seen as different from school and other organised activities and serve a different purpose in children's lives. Essentially children see play as the time they are not being organised by or told what to do by adults. Having this time is important to them as it gives them a chance to feel they have some autonomy and control in their otherwise frequently controlled lives.

Play is the time when children can meet and socialise with their friends, be physically active in relatively uncon-strained ways and choose to do as much or as little as they want. Children who feel happy and secure in their play can spend many hours occupied and enjoying themselves while at the same time investigating and learning about themselves and the world around them (NPFA and others 2000).

2.2.2 Play supports children's development, health and learning

Play and child development

Over many years play has been seen as an important part of children's development. While there is a significant body of research describing the value of play in the early development of children, there is little direct, empirical evidence on the benefits of play to school-aged children.

However, a combination of theoretical analyses, small scale studies and research into the views of play professionals and children and young people support the assertion that play is an important part of school-aged children's lives, which contributes to their social, physical, cultural, emotional and spiritual development (Street 2002).

A number of authors identify developmental and experiential advantages associated with children's play. These include the development of motivation and therefore participation in society, play's value in encouraging children to develop problem-solving skills, in supporting their language development and literacy, in developing their social skills and in expressing their emotions. Play is also seen as important in the development of children's imaginations and creative interests and abilities (Street 2002).

'Playing on the bikes, play indoors, do some painting and things.'

For children to get the maximum developmental and experiential benefit from their play, it appears they need to play in a variety of ways and be involved in different and distinctive types of play. Children themselves are very clear about their need and desire for a range of play opportunities and activities to be available to them (Cole-Hamilton 2002a).

'I like it a lot because it is not like school. The workers look after you but they don't act like teachers telling you what to do all the time. I think that's good. It makes me feel grown up.'

'My best thing is playing out I love it with my friends, I have learned how to climb and jump.'

Play and health

Physical health

The physical activity involved in energetic play is traditionally recognised as of benefit to children in terms of providing exercise. Although there has been little research directly linking play with levels of physical activity in children, research has shown that there are strong links between health status, physical activity, sport practice and level of fitness during childhood and adolescence (Street 2002).

Physical activity is widely recognised as an important health behaviour in childhood, providing benefits for both physical and psychological well-being. Physical benefits include positive effects for blood pressure and on preventing obesity which is rapidly becoming a major public health issue for children (Dietz 2001). Psychological effects include enhanced psychological well-being, reduced symptoms of depression and anxiety and increased self-esteem, and may be a protective factor against stress, depression and risk-taking behaviours such as drug use (Street 2002).

The few studies into the views of children about physical activity that do exist, suggest that physical activity is viewed positively by children and that the concept of 'being well' is commonly associated with being physically active and doing things. Crucially, although one study found very positive attitudes among children interviewed towards physical activities, their involvement in such activities was influenced by perceived enjoyment and of it being fun and by their parents' views of the facilities available. Parents

'My best thing is roller skating and also you get to play games like basketball and in the field you can play tennis and football.'

appear to play a central role in determining the levels of physical activity among their children and, in one of the studies of parents, a lack of facilities and play areas had a direct affect on the levels of physical activities engaged in by their children (Street 2002).

CPC's analysis of children's views about their play and free-time activities shows a widespread desire among children for more physically active sports and dance-based pursuits (Cole-Hamilton 2002a).

New research on brain activity based on animals is suggesting that play may activate higher cognitive processes and that there may be links between brain development and play. Other research, on physical activity levels, is also examining the effects on brain formation. Both issues are likely to stimulate further research which may shed valuable light on the importance of play (Street 2002).

Mental health

There is also a prevailing view that play can enhance the mental health of children and young people. This is particularly important given current concerns about increased rates of mental health problems among young people. Research highlights the importance of children being able to play and take risks and to use their own initiative. It also suggests that it is essential for them to have opportunities to practise making and consolidating friendships and to deal with conflict – the basic skills needed in order to become 'emotionally literate', which increases their resilience to mental health problems (Street 2002).

Children themselves also identify the opportunity to meet and spend time with their friends as one of the most important opportunities offered by play and play provision (Cole-Hamilton 2002a).

There may also be another aspect of play in supporting mental health, that of providing enriching experiences that may help to develop children's emotional and social skills

> 'I didn't want to go – my mum said I had to go because she was at work. But now I really like going. It's good and there's no teacher to nag you and stuff.'

and may reduce the risk of them developing mental health problems later on. Play gives children the chance to try out and experience a range of emotions, in a 'safe' way, allowing them to learn and develop emotionally. Research suggests that play may also may promote resilience where mention is made of 'spare time experiences' in helping to foster feelings of self-esteem and self-efficacy (Street 2002).

Children with specific needs

There appears to be little or no literature on the health benefits of play for disabled children and children from black and minority ethnic groups. This is an important omission given the particular concerns about the mental health needs of these groups of children and the research findings that these groups of young people experience more restricted access to their local environment, including to play and recreational provision (Street 2002). However, disabled children themselves are clear about the benefits to them of play provision (Cole-Hamilton 2002a).

> 'It's wicked. I can make space ships and everything.'

Play and learning

The educational benefits of play in the development of young children are well documented (Bruce 2001) and it is widely believed that the benefits of play to all children are wide ranging with particular implications for their emotional and social learning (Smith, S 2000).

In the education field, much of the literature has focused on the value of play in the learning of social skills and the formation of peer relationships and friendships. Play is seen to promote learning through giving control of their learning to the child and allowing them to learn through experience, repetition, rehearsal and problem solving, in their own ways and at their own pace. However, as researchers in this field acknowledge, even though the information which has been gathered is generally positive,

caution is needed since many of the studies are descriptive in their approach (Street 2002).

Analysis of teachers' perspectives of play in reception classes indicates that teachers value play within the curriculum. Play is seen as important in terms of language development and socialisation and can also reveal valuable information about a child's developmental stage, needs and interests. While there is a tension in meeting the demands of the National Curriculum, there are also other factors which have a role in constraining play opportunities in school, most especially large class sizes. The increasing use of play as a time management tool by teachers, and the reasons why they value play, require more extensive research (Street 2002).

A small body of literature suggests that children's views towards play are being influenced by a trend in society to devalue play as a medium for learning. However, much of the literature highlights their positive views towards playtime at school, in particular from the point of view of socialisation and making friends (Street 2002).

In two quite separate areas – folklore studies of children's play and research into the effects of exposure to arts and cultural learning activities – it appears that there is some useful recent data emerging which may support the importance of play activities in children's learning. Based on detailed case studies which explore the many aspects of children's play traditions and which examine children's actual play activities in the playground, and with an emphasis on children's own perceptions of play, according to the researchers working in this field, such studies provide a valuable source of data on the 'vibrancy, creativity and variety of free play activities'. The use of detailed case analysis also provides information on how

> 'I think play is very important to children as it teaches us colours and numbers and things.'

'I like it here because there's lots of friends'

children use play spaces, including the school playground, and 'the ways in which children learn and adapt games and rhymes in multicultural and monocultural settings' (Bishop and Curtis 2001, Street 2002).

No literature on the benefits of play and education for children with specific needs, disabled children and children from ethnic minority groups was identified during the review, a deficit which should be addressed as a part of any future research in this area (Street 2002).

'It's not like school as you get to do all sorts. I like baking the best. We're going to make cakes, will you help me?'

Play, socialisation and citizenship

Throughout the literature, a common theme is that play provides social benefits for children and young people in allowing them to mix with their peers and to exercise free choice. In doing so their self-confidence and feelings of self-worth are promoted. At this level, the assumed benefits are largely individual (Street 2002).

However, some of the recent literature on play takes another perspective – with some proponents of the importance of play arguing that it brings wider benefits to the community as a whole. By encouraging the use and development of local community facilities, play provision can have a strategic use in bringing more widespread social benefits including greater social cohesion and the building of community networks (Street 2002). This view was reinforced by play professionals responding to the CPC survey (Cole-Hamilton 2002b). Similarly, play provision which is able to give children access to computer technology, as much does today, can help prevent new social exclusions which Valentine and Holloway identified

as a result of the introduction of computer technology into schools and some homes (Valentine and Holloway 1999).

An overwhelming argument running through this literature is of the importance of effectively consulting with children and young people, in listening to their views and aspirations and in involving them in planning, particularly in urban areas (Street 2002).

2.2.3 The value of play provision to children, their families and the community

Although there has been little systematic, objective research into the value of different types of play provision to children, families and communities, the CPC survey of play professionals, and documented examples from elsewhere, show that over the last two years, a number of play projects have been funded as part of programmes aimed at improving local communities, indicating that the arguments for the benefits of play provision are being recognised in some areas.

The day-to-day experience of play professionals is that the provision they are involved in is important for the social lives of children, the social and economic lives of families and the well-being of communities.

The primary benefits of play provision for children are seen by play professionals to be the opportunity for them to socialise with other children, make new friends and have a good time. Also important are the health benefits, the feeling of security offered by the presence of staff and the opportunity to gain new experiences. Play provision is seen to:

- increase self-awareness, self-esteem, self-confidence and self-respect;

'It's so amazing, it gives you something to do and stops you getting bored.'

'I love it, it's really good. I just get bored at home so I have to go on at mum to let me come all the time.'

- give children the opportunity to mix with children from other backgrounds;
- allow children to increase in confidence through developing new skills;
- offer opportunities for socially excluded children to interact with others;
- offer good opportunities for social learning and interaction;
- allow children to make new friends from other areas.

Families are seen to be benefiting from children's play services which enable parents to work or train and ensure parents feel their children are happy, safe and enjoying themselves. Allowing parents the opportunity to have time away from their children is also seen as an important benefit of play provision. In addition, families are thought to benefit from having healthier, happier children. For many play professionals, the fact that their provision gave parents an opportunity to meet and socialise with other parents was also important.

Play provision is also seen as important in promoting community well-being and security. This is achieved by providing economic benefits, primarily through allowing parents to work and train and ensuring children are occupied and not becoming involved in anti-social behaviour. Buildings and facilities used by play services are frequently seen as a focal point for communities and play provision is thought to offer opportunities for social interaction for the wider community and to support the development of a greater sense of community spirit (Cole-Hamilton 2002b).

Community-based evaluations show that play projects lead to improvements in connections and trust in the local community. 'Prove it!', an approach to evaluation developed by the New Economics Foundation, Barclays plc and Groundwork UK, has been piloted in outside play and recreation spaces and showed a measurable impact on local interaction, new friendships, community know-how and community safety (New Economics Foundation 2001).

2.2.4 Play and playwork skills as valuable therapeutic tools

The importance of ensuring that children in hospital are offered good play opportunities is well established. However, there are a number of projects in England in which play and playwork skills are used to meet the very specific needs of small groups of children including children in homeless families, children with learning difficulties and behaviour that challenges and children whose families need specific types of support (Street 2002). For example:

- **Children in Temporary Accommodation Play (TAP) Project, Sheffield** – this project was established in 1998 with the aim of reducing stress within families living in temporary accommodation by providing play opportunities for children, and also to support the children in developing a range of skills.

- **The Building Bridges Project, supported by Camden Play Service** – this project provides a service for 5–13 year old children who have learning difficulties and challenging behaviour. All are referred to Building Bridges by the Local Education Authority (which is responsible for paying for the children's places within the project) with many also being known to social services and health agencies. The project offers what it describes as a 'very structured' play programme since the workers have found that the children respond well to short, focused pieces of activity. A key aim is to use play as a means of helping children to learn to manage their own behaviour.

- **The Kids and Co Group, Hollybush Family Centre Project, Hereford** – Hollybush Family Centre offers a variety of groups and support services to families with young children. One of its approaches is to help parents who missed out on experiences of play as a child, to have a chance to play and in doing so, to learn how to play with and relate positively with their child. Throughout the week, the centre offers a range of more structured groups, alongside more informal drop-in sessions. Discovering the importance of play is a key theme of the work undertaken (Street 2002).

- **Stamshaw Youth Support Project** – in 2000 Stamshaw Adventure Playground in Portsmouth ran a project to support victims of bullying from local schools, funded by Portsmouth City Council's Youth Service. Play workers from the playground ran the project which began with home visits to make an initial assessment for the young people and their parents. Staff aimed to develop an optimistic, no-blame approach among the young people in finding solutions to their problems. A getting to know each other game of bowling and a burger quickly followed up the home visits. This allowed staff to raise the subject of bullying to the group in an informal way and gave them the opportunity to observe the personalities within the group. Each session had an aim or theme although there was a flexibility that allowed staff to cut short or extend topics as necessary. Despite some minor set backs the project was largely successful with three out of the six noting significant improvements with regard to the amount of bullying they were experiencing.

2.3 Issues facing children's play provision in England

2.3.1 Children's views are not universally sought

Although there is increasing involvement of children and young people in the planning and development of their own play places, activities and opportunities (CPC 2002), this is far from universal. Data from Save the Children, cited by Adams and Ingham (1998), suggests that there is still a considerable way to go in terms of involving young people in planning for their local environment. This theme is also apparent in a number of pieces of research which have examined young peoples' experiences of town and city centres and their involvement in planning urban development (Davis and Jones 1997, Wheway and Millward 1997, Woolley and others 1999, Matthews and Limb 2000). Most recently, the Kids' Club Network report, *Looking to the Future for Children and Family: A Report of the*

Millennium Childcare Commission (KCN 2001), suggests that while there are now more examples of children being involved and consulted in service developments – for example, children's play zones and safe play areas – these tend to be examples of innovative good practice rather than standard practice (Street 2002).

Petrie and others' (2000b) examination of out of school provision, which is based on an in-depth analysis of a wide range of services for different user groups and interviews with both professionals and families, reaches similar conclusions. She suggests that 'congenial and realistic ways of consulting with children need to be found. Perhaps more importantly, we may need to recast how we think about children: not as needy recipients or consumers of services, but as participants, with other children and adults, within services'. This theme is echoed in recent work by Moss (2000) who notes that in Britain, 'the surveillance, control and regulation of children are dominant' (Street 2002).

If children do not like open access play provision, they do not use it. However, children using formal childcare provision do not have the same choice and are reliant for their play opportunities on those who organise and run the provision. Although much of the consultation and participation work involving children asks for their views and opinions on service and planning developments, it does not actively involve them in these processes.

2.3.2 Play opportunities are under threat in many areas

A number of studies describe a reduction in children's use of the outdoors over the past few decades. This appears to be mostly as result of increased urbanisation, more and faster traffic, parental fears of real and perceived dangers and children's fears of bullies. It is also due in part to the emergence of attractive indoor activities. Evidence also indicates that there has been a steady reduction in play

'Go to the park – it's rubbish.'

'In the park there is only a slide and a climbing frame. Other things are too far away.'

space including playing fields, open spaces and play-grounds, over the last 20 years. This reduction in outdoor play activity has occurred at the same time as children and young people in the UK have become more sedentary and when among primary school children in particular, levels of physical activity are declining (Street 2002).

At the same time, there are concerns that within the education system, children are under more and more pressure, with the opportunities for free play being increasingly squeezed out or down-graded in learning value (Carvel 1999, Macintyre 2001). Overall, as society becomes more complex and competitive, there is concern that spontaneous play is being replaced with structured activities both at home and within school (Rogers and Sawyers 1988, Mental Health Foundation 1999).

Play opportunities have also been being curtailed by a loss of space, the increasing commodification of leisure, heightened parental fears for the safety of their children and a growing sense of increased control over children's lives (Street 2002). One research study shows that opportunities for play for children in London have been found to be restricted by a number of factors including: societal fears for children's safety in public spaces; the increasing prominence of the Government's education agenda in the lives of children; the effects of poverty, disadvantage and discrimination on children's access to play and leisure services and failures to address income-based inequalities (Hood 2001).

Use of provision by children who are disabled or have specific needs has also been found to be decreasing in the recent past. In 2000 the proportion of out-of-school clubs used by disabled children was found to be in decline with only 21 per cent of the clubs surveyed being used by disabled children (Smith, F 2000).

'There is playground near us but it is full of broken glass and burnt cars – we don't go there.'

One study has also found that transfer of resources from open access playschemes to formal childcare has the potential to affect children from, for example, Pakistani and Bangladeshi communities which are among the poorest in Britain. Research with Asian families has shown that families living in poverty could not afford to pay for childcare and, as more and more open access play projects were becoming fee paying childcare schemes, Asian children, particularly from low income families, were being denied access to play opportunities. In one of the areas surveyed the local authority had to close an open access adventure playground used by around 70 children in the evenings during term time, and open a number of fee paying childcare facilities instead. This had adversely affected the local Asian community (Kapasi 2001).

2.3.3 Children want challenge, providers are worried about liability

Many children and young people want exciting, challenging play opportunities with a degree of risk. This can be at odds with the concerns of providers, who may be more worried about liability in the event of accidents (Moorcock 1998) – a fear which may be fuelled by the growth in legal actions concerned with compensation for personal accident injuries. There is also anecdotal evidence that public liability insurance premiums for play provision are increasing.

2.3.4 'Postcode play'

The availability of children's play opportunities depends on where they live. The exercise in mapping children's play provision undertaken as part of the Children's Play Council research programme indicated significant variations in play provision in the 16 West Midlands local authority areas for which information was available. There were also very wide variations in funding with some authorities spending ten times as much as others per play area and over four times as much per child (Harrop 2002).

> 'The parks are dirty and not enough equipment, people leave needles there, it's dangerous.'

Unsupervised play areas

Among the local authorities in the West Midlands mapping exercise, the average (median) number of unsupervised play areas was one for every 370 children aged between 5 and 16, ranging from one for every 170 children in one area to one for every 1,600 in another. The average (median) level of spending was about £4 per child per year, ranging from £1.70 to £7.50. In one quarter of cases the local authority was not the main provider of play areas. In other authorities both levels of spending and number of play areas varied considerably, although the two did not always go hand-in-hand. Some higher spending authorities had relatively few, well-resourced play areas, and some lower spending authorities had relatively numerous, under-resourced areas (Harrop 2002).

> 'The swings are missing, the council came and took them away, we don't know where to.'

Supervised play provision

Among the 16 authorities, many council officers reported having little knowledge of the activities of other providers of supervised play provision such as schools, voluntary organisations and other tiers of local government. Often, reported information only covered provision funded or delivered by the local authority.

The average (median) number of supervised play settings was one for every 630 children, while the average (median) level of spending was about £5.20 per child per year. Three-quarters of the authorities supplied incomplete information for provision not funded by the council. This finding reinforces the earlier finding that, despite the expansion of childcare and study support, and the development of EYDCPs, NOF consortium bids, Cultural Strategies and community planning, local authorities are not always well linked into wider out-of-school provision.

Despite some discrepancies in reporting, there are large variations in the quantity and characteristics of supervised play provision funded by different local authorities. The highest spending unitary authority spends ten times as much per child as the lowest, while the highest spending district council spends more than ten times as much per child as the lowest. These variations were related to differences in both the places available in each supervised play setting, and the council's spending per setting.

A quarter of local authorities reported there were local adventure playgrounds. All but one reported that term-time provision exists, with around half of councils funding some provision. Holiday schemes were also known to exist in all but one authority.

> 'They just say what we want to do and they have exciting activities on offer. The week before they write it down what we want to do.'

2.3.5 Age and gender: different needs and wishes

As children get older they begin to move further away from home as they play. Their interests change and their physical and mental capacity is extended. It is frequently these older children whose play needs are not being adequately met. For example one study found that children over nine years old were not happy in clubs with much younger children but were happiest in clubs where they had their own space and where there were activities more appropriate to their age (Smith, F 2000). Similarly the CPC review of children's consultations found that children

> 'No things for teenagers to do after school – there is nowhere to go, you just hang around the streets.'

'Most of my friends are older than me, they are 12 and they don't come anymore. I don't know why, I think it's because of the age groups and they are too old.'

from 11 to 16 years of age were most likely to feel there was little or nothing for them to do in their spare time (Cole-Hamilton 2002a).

Although older children's needs are different from those of their younger brothers and sisters, they are frequently called on to look after the younger children. In some areas, therefore, providing for play means making sure that there are suitable, attractive play opportunities for different groups of children within sight of each other. However, creating provision suitable for mixed age groups takes imagination, consultation and resources. In one study of children's use of commercial playgrounds, young children thought that older children were a danger and older children thought that younger children were a danger in the playground. Although the children interviewed enjoyed playing in the playgrounds they thought they would enjoy themselves more if the play equipment was more challenging. Adults, on the other hand, were more concerned with making playgrounds safer (McKendrick 2000).

Girls and boys also tend to choose different types of activity and the CPC review indicated that girls were more likely to enjoy physical activities such as dance and drama while boys tended to prefer more sports-based activities (Cole-Hamilton 2002a).

2.3.6 Groups of children denied play opportunities

Children who are disabled or have specific needs

Published research suggests that access to play and out-of-school services for disabled children is frequently difficult, often because of insufficient funding which is

likely to be a reflection of underfunded play services generally (Petrie and others 2000a). While providers describe themselves as willing to include disabled children, attitudes and lack of awareness are often a major stumbling block to disabled children's access to play opportunities (Petrie and others 2000b).

Even though local authorities might recognise disabled children as having the same right to play as others, in practice their access to out-of-school services is more limited.

This is partly because 'including' disabled children in mainstream play provision is perceived to require extra resources especially if there is a need for higher staffing ratios. There is also considerable variability in the amount of equipment in play provision suitable for and attractive to disabled children.

In a survey conducted by Mencap in Dudley, many parents of disabled children said they depended on playschemes as the primary focus for their children's activities in the school holidays. However, service providers cited the extra costs they might incur on access and equipment and the need for high staff-child ratios as reasons why providing more inclusive holiday provision was difficult (Attfield 2001).

Opportunities for disabled and non-disabled children to play together in mainstream provision are especially important as, in both mainstream and special schools, disabled children spend the vast majority of their time in the company of adults rather than other children (Watson and others 2000).

There are many factors that restrict play opportunities for disabled children. One of these is physical access. Many playgrounds are still inaccessible or provide only

'There should be older groups because at the moment there is 8–13 years. My mum works so I would have to stay at home by myself and it gets really boring. And we are in with 8 year olds who can't kick a ball. I'd like a 12 and up group – 12 to 15 year olds.'

inaccessible equipment. Frequently, poor design of equipment and inadequate maintenance means that most unsupervised play areas are not only inaccessible, they actively discourage disabled children from sharing in the fun (CPC and others 2001). Difficult physical access to playgrounds reduces opportunities for disabled children to meet and socialise with friends (Watson 2000).

Where local authorities provide specialist 'Special Educational Needs (SEN) Summer Schemes', these frequently have minimal play value. In the view of the inclusive play agency Kidsactive, 'Rather than *managing* large numbers of children with complex impairments in segregated provision, experienced workers could work with children at local playschemes' (Maddocks 2001). The transport requirements of bussing children to specialist schemes also increase the perceived cost of providing play opportunities for disabled children.

As a result, disabled children's autonomy is more circumscribed than that of other children. Where good inclusive provision for disabled children does exist, it allows them the opportunity to play, often to be physically active and, for many, to interact with their peers.

Children from black and minority ethnic communities

Studies looking specifically at how the needs of children from different black and minority ethnic groups are addressed in play and out-of-school provision indicate that, in some areas, children do not use existing provision because they feel it is not suitable for them. In some instances children describe experiencing racism accompanied by inadequate awareness and training of staff to deal appropriately with this (Street 2002).

'When I lived in Bangladesh I used to like playing tig tig, splashing the water and hide and seek. I miss playing in the sand.'

Research with Asian children and their families and play projects found that Asian children sometimes preferred to play out on the streets rather than in staffed playplaces. This was because the children did not feel comfortable using the play projects and did not feel a sense of belonging. In two play projects, situated in the areas with large Asian populations but underused by Asian children, there were no images of Asian people and many parents said these projects were not for their children because there were no such images (Kapasi 2001).

In the survey of Asian children's play opportunities, some of the workers understood that racism was a large factor in Asian children not using local provision. Their projects were based in communities where racist language and behaviour was a part of everyday life and they had to work hard to overcome this major barrier. However, this was not always the case and some white playworkers did not feel racism to be an issue in their projects, even though the research identified that children and families were aware of it (Kapasi 2001).

Some groups of children may also be being denied access to play provision because it does not meet the cultural expectations of their families. Kapasi found that while the average attendance in mainstream provision was about 25 per cent Asian girls and 75 per cent Asian boys, in most cases only a handful of Asian girls attended play projects regularly with very few new girls joining. Availability of transport for girls' groups increased use of provision by girls (Kapasi 2001).

Kapasi also found that the most successful groups to reach Asian children were community-led schemes. However, these were frequently marginalised and unsupported (Kapasi 2001).

In another study of the way in which children from black and minority ethnic communities in London access and use play provision, it emerged that waiting lists and restrictions on the numbers of children able to attend play projects meant that some children were unable to use the provision. Although this affected all children, it had particular implications for children from black and minority ethnic communities, who frequently wanted to attend play projects with friends because of their fears of potential racism. If the provision was unable to accommodate a whole group of friends, the children were less likely to use the projects (Kapasi 2002).

Children in families with low incomes

The recent expansion of childcare has, in some areas, led to a shift in the balance between childcare and play provision, with open access play provision being replaced by childcare. From the CPC analysis of research with parents it is clear that parents with low incomes are the least likely to be using childcare. It is of concern, therefore, that in some areas the play opportunities of children in low income families might be becoming eroded (Cole-Hamilton 2002b).

This concern was borne out in the four case study authorities, where the majority of supervised provision was paid for. With the exception of council-funded clubs in one rural district council, independent summer play-schemes in the other and play centres in one of the urban unitary authorities, almost all staffed provision was run on a childcare basis, with children being registered for a whole session (Harrop 2002).

> 'You can only go once a week cos it costs, and you have to pay bus fares too.'

Refugee children

Research suggests that refugee children have fewer friends at school and among their neighbours than their non-refugee peers, and often do not pursue leisure activities that involve money, such as going to the cinema. For many, the education system seems to be the only statutory agency from which they derive support in settling into their new lives. Refugee children are also less likely to visit friends and relatives, spend time outside with friends and go window shopping than other children, which suggests that their opportunities for free play are also curtailed (Candappa 2000).

Traveller children

Traveller children from a number of sites in the south west of England, when consulted about their 'dream site', overwhelmingly felt that they lacked and wanted proper play spaces on their sites. They identified equipment such as swings and slides and places to ride their bikes and build tree houses as some of the most important improvements they would make (Hughes 1998).

Children in rural areas

For children living in rural areas, there is frequently nowhere to play except in and around their homes (Stobart 1992). It can also be difficult for children who have to travel to have contact with their friends. Valentine found that the parents of children in rural England were so concerned for their children's safety that they heavily supervised their children's use of space. Children's free play and independent environmental exploration was constrained as their parents acted as chauffeurs for them and their friends, taking them to organised activities. Free play in the countryside was also restricted by changes in farming practices (Valentine 1997).

Matthews and Limb also found that children living in rural villages often felt excluded and powerless within their communities. Many felt dislocated from village life and felt a strong sense of alienation with few places to go and little for them to do (Matthews and Limb 2000).

2.3.7 Lack of planning and support

Strategic planning, based on a corporate play policy, is important if all children are to have access to a range of quality play opportunities. However, the mapping exercise undertaken as part of the CPC research programme shows that strategic development for play in England is inconsistent and frequently non-existent.

Information was collected relating to 167 of 391 local authorities (43 per cent). This showed that, of the local authorities for which information was available:

- 42 per cent had a dedicated play officer;
- 34 per cent had play services;
- 37 per cent had play policy documents;
- 42 per cent had plans or strategies for developing play opportunities;
- associations or networks supporting play were reported to be operating in 70 per cent of local authorities.

These figures are almost certainly an overestimate as it is likely that local authorities with an active play sector are more likely to be known to the regional play experts providing the information for the survey. For example, an unpublished survey of readers of *Play Today* undertaken by CPC in 2001 indicated that there were play associations and networks in fewer than 60 per cent of local authorities.

The development of strategic planning for play varied within and between the English regions with London having the largest known proportion of authorities with play officers, services, policies and plans (Harrop 2002).

2.3.8 Quality control and assurance

Agreed quality assurance mechanisms are needed to ensure consistency and equality of opportunity for children's play. But quality control and assurance in children's play provision varies widely across the country.

Regulation and inspection

Play services are currently widely inspected under the provisions of the Children Act 1998 and health and safety legislation. The CPC survey of play professionals showed that, of the 176 respondents, over 90 per cent said their service or provision was subject to regular inspection. Of these, 71 per cent were inspected under the Children Act 1989 and 7 per cent under health and safety legislation. In addition:

- 28 services (17 per cent) described regular, internal, physical inspection of equipment – these almost all involved unsupervised play provision;
- 19 services (12 per cent) had their own local standards and guidelines; and
- 14 (9 per cent) were subject to Ofsted inspections.

A small number of services were subject to inspections by their grant-giving body and one scheme was inspected by the EYDCP.

Sixteen of the respondents were involved in provision or services that were not subject to inspection. While some of these were support services, others did have direct contact with children. Reasons for not being subject to inspection included the local authority having a policy of not inspecting open access provision and the provision being outside the legal scope of the Children Act inspections (Cole-Hamilton 2002b).

Quality Assurance (QA) schemes

In 2000, although inspections were extensive, internal quality assurance schemes were less widely used. In the CPC survey of play professionals, of the 182 people answering the question:

- 32 per cent used formal QA schemes;
- 32 per cent were in the process of developing schemes; and
- 36 per cent did not use QA schemes.

Of those using or developing QA schemes, 42 per cent had their own local schemes, frequently based on the PQASSO scheme and 25 per cent used *Aiming High*, published by Kids' Clubs Network. Other schemes included *Quality in Play* (Conway and Farley 2001) and the then draft *Play Wales* document, now published as *The First Claim* (Play Wales 2001). Two in three respondents said that the children who used the service or provision were formally involved in evaluation or monitoring (Cole-Hamilton 2002b).

New QA schemes, which emphasise the value and nature of play, are currently developed by some local authorities and need to be fully evaluated in the future.

Performance indicators

In the West Midlands mapping exercise, five of the 16 authorities had targets or local performance indicators for play provision and another was currently preparing indicators for a new programme. The most commonly collected information related to play areas' compliance with the Six Acre Standard (NPFA 2001) and attendance information for supervised play provision. Two of the councils had internal quality assurance programmes. The other two councils measured performance using indicators which measured levels of use (Harrop 2002).

Best Value

In 2000, awareness of Best Value reviews was high with almost all those working in local authorities knowing their service would be reviewed if it had not already been. Among the voluntary organisations represented in the responses, 11 play associations and local voluntary providers were aware of Best Value reviews in their areas, including one in which the review was complete, three where the review was in progress and seven where the review was planned (Cole-Hamilton 2002b).

In the two rural areas investigated in the case study research, Best Value reviews were not yet scheduled. However, in both urban areas reviews had been undertaken: in one, a cross-cutting review of all services for children, and in the other, supervised provision delivered by Community Education (Harrop 2002).

2.3.9 Staffing issues

There are wide variations in the way local providers support and develop their playwork workforce. Playwork is highly skilled, requiring an unusual combination of skills as well as an ability to understand children and their free-time needs. But in general, it was evident from the CPC consultation process and play policy seminars, that wages are low, recruitment and retention difficult and staff frequently feel undervalued. Many playwork staff are employed on short-term contracts and part-time work is the norm. Significant numbers of staff work across services for children and young people working in early years settings some of the time, in youth work, as assistants in schools and then in out-of-school and holiday provision for the remainder. This has major implications for training and conditions of service, with staff working to a number of different managers, having limited opportunities for proper training and limited access to appraisal and career development opportunities.

In the CPC case study research all four local authorities identified recruitment, retention and training issues as key challenges for improving play provision. In all the areas, term-time recruitment was difficult both for local authorities and independent providers, because of short, awkward working hours and low pay. In all four authorities, planning documents set out plans or policies for the training of playworkers, while two set out plans for recruitment (Harrop 2002). In the play policy seminars run by CPC the need to develop and value a skilled workforce was seen as one of the primary issues.

In the three case study local authorities that provided services, all workers received some level of training, although only in one authority were all workers expected to have a playwork NVQ. In two of the authorities there were a handful of people with Level 3 NVQs. Limited information was available about the level of training of workers in independent provision, although there were some qualified playworkers in each area.

Approaches to resolving workforce problems in the case study areas included: creating packages of work at several sites of provision; introducing flexible rotas; and offering competitive pay. For independent providers, the most significant challenge was meeting training needs, with

'The staff don't get paid enough.'

'Workers should be kind, responsible, funny, strict when they have to be and have a first aid qualification.'

many lacking the capacity to train staff themselves. In the two urban authorities this problem was being addressed through free training from EYDCPs (although levels of take-up were unclear) while one of the districts had a training programme for potential workers. For local authorities, retention was something of a problem, with trained workers moving on to new careers or into independent provision (in the latter case, admittedly, staying in the local pool of trained workers) (Harrop 2002). Training in inclusive play is also a positive way of adding value and developing the workforce.

2.3.10 Funding issues

Local funding for children's play comes from a large number of sources (see Appendix 4, page 68) and is often not well coordinated at local level. Individuals, projects, partnerships, neighbourhood groups and local government departments apply to a myriad of funds for resourcing play provision with, in some areas, little systematic coordination or planning between fundraisers. Much of the funding given is for capital investment or short-term 'pilot' or 'start-up' projects with little thought being given to long-term sustainability.

The income generation potential of most play provision, especially in economically deprived areas, is very low and careful planning is needed to meet on-going running and maintenance costs.

The West Midlands mapping process indicated that in:

Unsupervised play areas – there was clear disparity in the amount local authorities spent on each play area. In the urban areas variations in spending in part mirrored the significant variations in the number of play areas in the two authorities. In the two districts the local authority was not the main funder of play areas.

Supervised play provision – there was some relationship between authorities' spending and the number of play provision settings each operated. But other factors which influenced variations in spending were the duration and style of different authorities' provision.

While both levels of spending and number of play areas varied considerably, the two did not always go hand-in-hand. Some higher spending authorities had relatively few, well-resourced play areas, and some lower spending authorities had relatively numerous, under-resourced areas. Detailed analysis of the 12 authorities who were the main providers of play areas suggested they could be divided into the following four groups:

- Few play areas, each with high funding resulting in high/medium spending per child (4 authorities).
- Few play areas, each with low/medium funding resulting in low spending per child (3 authorities).
- Many play areas, each with low funding resulting in low spending per child (2 authorities).
- Many play areas, each with medium funding resulting in high spending per child (3 authorities).

As already noted, in supervised play provision the highest spending unitary authority spent ten times per child population as much as the lowest, and the highest spending district council spent more than ten times as much as the lowest (Harrop 2002).

2.3.11 Research into play and school-aged children

The CPC-commissioned review of published literature (Street 2002) identified widespread activity in both research and service development where play may be a component of what is provided. In particular, within the academic fields of geography and urban studies, research interest was apparent in children's use of and access to urban spaces, their use of commercial play spaces and the 'commodification' of childhood.

There is also a substantial body of literature which examines in some depth the various theories of play, and which is drawn from a range of different disciplines, including child psychology and child psychotherapy, human geography, anthropology and studies of children's folklore. Traditionally these have focused on benefits to the individual child; more recently, the focus has been on benefits to society as a whole.

Alongside this, a variety of studies have examined the issue of risk, both from the perspectives of children and their parents, and how this may curtail their access to play provision located outside the home. Another reasonably frequent line of inquiry has focused on children's participation in the planning of provision and their access to and experience of their local environment. The quality of provision, guidelines for promoting safety, for ensuring inclusion in play and encouraging access for disabled children, have also been the subject of published reports (Street 2002).

Studies examining the growth of structured out-of-school provision, including learning or study support, the changing role of schools and the impact of such provision on children, and the place for play within the national curriculum, are a further developing focus of investigation.

However, while there is widespread recognition and discussion of the importance of play in the health and development of school-aged children, empirical evidence is harder to come by. For example:

- Much of the research is focused on the pre-school and younger age group, with less attention on adolescents.

- There remains a lack of systematic outcome analysis, most especially on a longitudinal basis.

- The definitions used for play are often imprecise and the boundaries between play, sport, learning and education remain poorly defined.

- The sample sizes used in research studies are often small and very local in their focus.

- Data about young people from minority ethnic groups, those who are disabled or have other special needs (for example, excluded from school or homeless) remains generally sparse.

- The struggle to keep up with running a project and the need continually to search for funding, means that many innovative projects have not been able to undertake systematic evaluation (Street 2002).

2.4 UK perspectives

2.4.1 Wales

During 2000/2001 the National Assembly for Wales (NAFW) developed a number of initiatives to support the development of children's play opportunities in Wales. These included:

- Play 2000 grant: Early in the year the Play 2000 grant was launched. This initiative focused specifically on open access play provision. Local Children and Youth Partnerships were given £1,000,000 to spend, across Wales, on open access play provision. This grant has now been extended into 2001/02 and beyond.

- Commissioning Play Wales to undertake a review of open access provision in Wales and to document the way in which the Play 2000 grant was being utilised by local partnerships. The review was coordinated by Play Wales, the Wales Local Government Association, and the National Assembly for Wales, and in December 2000 the *State of Play 2000* report and recommendations (Play Wales 2000) were accepted by the Health and Social Services Committee.

2.4.2 Scotland

A new commitment to children's play is also emerging in Scotland. There is now a major emphasis on the importance of services to children and young people in Scotland. In 2001 the document *For Scotland's Children – better integrated children's services* (Scottish Executive 2001) set the scene for Play Scotland to be able to emphasise the value of play for children and young people.

The Scottish Executive has agreed core funding for Play Scotland for the next three years and they are now in a position to implement long-term plans and concentrate on providing advice and information to members as well as continually promoting the value of play through developing publications and information briefings.

2.4.3 Northern Ireland

PlayBoard Northern Ireland (PBNI) has a pivotal role in the development of play and childcare provision in Northern Ireland. As an Intermediary Funding Body (IFB) for the second round of funding from the EU Programme for Peace and Reconciliation, it is distributing a £3 million package to PlayClubs offering out-of-school play provision for children, which in turn enables their parents to access training, education and employment opportunities.

As an IFB under the Peace I (the first funding round), PlayBoard funded around 100 clubs. Over 2000 children have benefited, over 250 playworkers have been employed and almost 200 NVQs in Playwork have been supported by the agency. IFB status under Peace II allows PlayBoard to continue promoting this work by continuing to support existing PlayClubs and help establish new provision.

Priorities for the PBNT include:

- To assist local councils in developing play policies and strategies, in partnership with local communities.

- To work with government departments with a remit for children's play to deliver on the commitment in their Programme for Government to develop strategies for play, in partnership with local councils, the community and voluntary sector. Statutory responsibility for children's play in Northern Ireland is not the responsibility of one single government department. It is an overarching issue and many departments have a particular remit for a single component of play policy and provision.

- To assist local communities in taking forward plans for traffic calming measures and home zones in order to secure safe play opportunities for children in the streets where they live.

- To continue assisting the Office of the First Minister and Deputy First Minister in the creation of an office of Commissioner for Children for Northern Ireland and the development of the Northern Ireland Children's Strategy, of which play should be an over-arching issue.

Section 3: The future for children's play

'Please do something about our area because we are all classed as delinquents but we are not. We want somewhere to go. Thank you.'

Providing for play must start with children, and with listening to their needs and wishes. Parents and others in the community also need to be involved and supportive. Local authorities and partnerships of different kinds are key local delivery agencies. Central Government has an essential role in providing strategic leadership through giving guidance, supporting the development of standards, providing and shaping funding and supporting infrastructure and support agencies and mechanisms.

This section puts forward 56 recommendations for action, aimed at local, regional and national agencies from both statutory and voluntary sectors. All can be implemented without radical new structures or changes in legislation. The tools are already largely in place for improving play opportunities for children, locally, regionally and nationally. But these tools can and should be made to work much more effectively. The recommendations draw on consultations with play professionals across England. Many build on existing initiatives and emerging good practice.

There are seven key recommendations, highlighted in **bold type**, which underpin many of the others. They emphasise the need for strategic direction and focus, coupled with resources, at national and local levels.

Section 2.3 of this report highlights some of the current problems and barriers to the development of universally good play opportunities for all children and young people in England. However, there is also a considerable amount of existing and developing good and innovative practice which needs to be recognised and promoted. This section includes case studies showing what is already being done and what can be developed and built upon across England.

3.1 Listening to children and providing the play opportunities they want and need

Although the participation of children in the development of play opportunities is far from universal, there are many examples of interesting practice. The variety and extent and nature of children's involvement was evident in the CPC survey of play professionals and in the review of consultations with children and young people. Examples of consulting with children include:

- workshops, seminars and fora;
- questionnaire surveys and needs assessment;
- children's Taster Days;
- large scale, randomised surveys;

- dedicated children's participation projects;
- village appraisals and involving children and young people;
- children/family events – e.g. National Playday;
- regular children's meetings and small-scale surveys (Cole-Hamilton 2002a and 2002b).

In the West Midlands mapping, conducted by the New Policy Institute, 13 of 16 authorities had recently consulted with children, as had all four of the case study areas (Harrop 2002).

CASE STUDY 2 Cheltenham Children's Rights Conference

For six months, in early 2001, 35 children and young people, in four groups, consulted other local children about their rights, especially in relation to their free-time activities. Each group was involved in constructing questionnaires, interviewing children and young people, collating the data and preparing and delivering a conference speech. Each group was supported by an adult worker who offered support and guidance as required.

In June 2001 the four groups of young consultants presented their findings to a conference of adult providers and policy makers. Also, at the conference was a display from a local early years group showing the equipment the children would like to see in their perfect play area.

The presentations showed in pictures, anecdotes and statistics, where children play, in and around Cheltenham, and what problems they face in trying to find safe, interesting places to play outside. Identifying children's play needs with and by children and young people in this way has proved invaluable to the Play Development Service in informing its future planning for improved play opportunities for children and young people.

CASE STUDY 3 'Playing for Real' with devon@play

In Devon, several play areas have been developed using the 'Playing for Real' process, inspired by the 'Planning for Real' planning technique, using physical models as a basis for discussion.

At the request of the local community a devon@play worker visits the site with a group of local children. The children explain what they like and dislike about the site, how they access it and what they wish to do when they play there. The group then go to an indoor venue where there is a short discussion and an opportunity to look at varied display material. Questionnaires are given to the children, which they are helped to complete if necessary.

The practical session begins with a 'map' of the play area being set out either on cloth, sand or clean compost. The children then create models, from modelling and scrap materials, of features and equipment they would like to see on the site. Finally, the model is discussed and a consensus reached on the most important aspects of the design.

The playworker uses this information to write a report given to the community, parish council or local authority to incorporate into the final plan.

'Playing for Real' draws children together to discuss and plan, uncovering local solutions. It adds credibility to the planning group (useful if there is local opposition) and helps break down barriers as it is accessible to children who find it difficult to express themselves. 'Playing for Real' improves the organisation's knowledge of local action and provides contacts in sometimes remote rural locations. The team have experienced no negative reactions to the process; people say it is informative and are impressed by the contribution of the children. Play areas which incorporate children's views tend to be well used and looked after by the children themselves, have fewer problems with vandalism, and can even cost less than areas designed solely by adults.

The Children's Rights Conference held in Cheltenham (see Case study 2) and the 'Playing for Real' consultations undertaken in Devon (see Case study 3) show two different but successful methods of consulting with children and young people about their play and free-time activities.

If children and young people are to be allowed and encouraged to describe and define their own needs for play and free time activities there needs to be:

- Commitment from local authorities, partnerships and other providers to seek out children and young people, listen to their views and act on their expressed needs and wishes.

- A determined effort by local authority planning and development agencies to consult local children and young people about any decision which might affect their opportunities to play.

- Appropriate and informed techniques to include children and young people from under-represented groups, in particular disabled children, in consultation processes.

- Recognition in schools that opportunities for play during the school day are an important element of children's education and that children should be involved in discussions about play time and play-time activities.

- Recognition and an understanding of the value of play by childcare staff and providers to ensure that they allow children the opportunity to define their own play needs.

- Systematic implementation and careful monitoring of the Government's core principles for involving children and young people.

We therefore recommend that

Action	Agencies
1 Local authority, partnership and other local agency staff involved in community consultations automatically include children and young people in any consultation process involving change, that they seek out children who might not automatically come forward to take part and that they ensure they have consulted with children from all ages groups whose play opportunities might be affected by the proposed changes.	Local authorities, partnerships and other local agencies
2 Local planning, development and renewal agencies and partnerships are expected to consider children's views about their play needs in any new or re-developments.	DTLR (guidance) Local agencies
3 Local quality assurance systems monitor the extent and impact of the involvement of children and young people in local planning, development and regeneration.	Audit Commission Best Value Performance Indicators (BVPIs)
4 Schools work closely with pupils, playground staff and specialist organisations such as Learning Through Landscapes to develop their play times and outside spaces for children's play.	Individual schools
5 Children's involvement in decisions that affect their play free-time activities becomes an integral part of any evaluation of the CYPU's Core Principles.	CYPU

3.2 Gaining support from parents and carers

Whatever the range of play opportunities available to children and young people, they will only be able to make full use of them if their parents and carers allow them to. Parents must feel sure their children are safe and be confident they will not come to harm.

Parents themselves are concerned about the opportunities for their children to play. In an opinion poll conducted for CPC in 1999, although nearly 70 per cent of parents worried that their children's development was suffering from poor outside play opportunities, nearly 80 per cent said one of the main reasons their child did not play outside was because they feared for their the child's safety. Nearly one in three said that the lack of playgrounds in local parks stopped their children playing outside and one in four said playgrounds were too dirty and equipment unsafe (Cole-Hamilton 2002a). In some areas, for example in Southwark in London, parents are working closely with local planners and neighbourhood renewal teams to address the play needs of local children (see Case study 4).

If parents and informal carers of children are to understand and appreciate the value of play to their children, be sure their children are safe from harm, and support and be involved in the development of improved play opportunities in their local communities, there needs to be:

- places for children to play where their parents can feel confident they are safe and enjoying themselves;
- encouragement and support to parents involved in community initiatives to develop and improve children's play opportunities;
- information in parenting programmes about the nature and importance of play for children of all ages as they grow and develop.

CASE STUDY 4 Little Dorrit Playground, Southwark: local parents lead the way

Little Dorrit Park in Bankside, London was first opened in 1902. It was created as an area specifically for children to play in a part of town notorious for its brothels, warehouses and destitution. This history spurred a local group of parents and other volunteers into redeveloping a piece of ground that had fallen into disrepair. The ground itself is surrounded by offices but has two nearby primary schools and a lot of Local Authority housing close by.

Southwark Council provided the majority of the funding through Capital Funding, while additional funds were raised through projects such as the Millennium Arts Project (£5,000), and local fundraising and small grants. In total they obtained upwards of £50,000.

The group began by consulting with local children in the area through after-school parties, and big events within the park. At these events, which over 500 local children attended, entertainers and arts and crafts people were present, and the main consultation was in the form of a series of boards on which various pictures of play equipment (previously shortlisted by the group) were attached. The children were given stickers to stick on their favourite pieces of equipment, which were described by activity rather than by technical terms. The group also used the Bankside Open Spaces Trust young people's consultation project for 10–12 year olds.

The group also got advice from the council's landscape designer and the equipment that had been selected by the group for the exercise was chosen for its low cost, durability and safety.

The play space has had almost no vandalism since it opened in 2000. The group feels that this is because local families were involved throughout its design and the community are proud of what they see as their facility.

We therefore recommend that

Action	Agencies
6 Local authorities and agencies with an interest in play work closely with Community Safety networks, parks departments, and highways and traffic departments to improve safety in open public and play spaces.	Relevant local authority departments and agencies, parents and carers groups
7 Community development initiatives aimed at capacity building seek out and encourage the involvement of parents and carers interested in developing children's play opportunities.	Local community development agencies
8 Parenting programmes include information, advice and training about children's play.	Parent support and advice networks

3.3 Winning over the community

If children's play opportunities are not to be limited by hostility from some adults in the local community, considerable work needs to be done to persuade all local residents of the importance and benefits of play to the whole community. They need to understand that children have the same right to public spaces as they do. That children need to play and benefit from play and that providing good, attractive play opportunities is good for the whole community as well.

Building community support and acceptance may involve:

- Education programmes aimed at adults in local communities about the value and importance of providing children with places where they can play freely and without interference from adults.

- Community planning and consultation groups which bring children, young people, and different groups of adults together to discuss and learn about each other's needs, wishes and fears.

- Local programmes which help to mediate between different groups and interests within the community.

We therefore recommend that

Action	Agencies
9 A programme of public information dissemination is developed which informs the public of the value of play to children, families and communities.	DCMS, play sector, EYDCPs, Children's Information Service (CIS), DfES, parents' groups
10 Successful projects are identified and promoted where intergenerational consultation groups and projects mediating between children and young people and older community members exist.	DCMS, play sector, community development sector
11 Links are created with organisations representing the views and interest of older people and people from different community groups to develop common areas of work on promoting community harmony.	Play sector, voluntary organisations representing other community groups

3.4 Ensuring good local play opportunities for all

The views of local children and young people, support from parents who feel that their children will be safe from harm, and an appreciation from community members of the importance of allowing children a range of play opportunities are the primary building blocks for successful play provision. The onus is then on local authorities, strategic and other partnerships and other agencies to ensure that a suitable range of opportunities is developed, provided and maintained. For this to be achieved, local planners and providers need to:

- work together to an agree set of values and principles (Section 3.4.1);
- provide play opportunities which meet the needs of all local children (Section 3.4.2);
- develop and support a strong infrastructure for children's play (Section 3.4.3);
- monitor and promote high standards through quality assurance and inspection regimes (Section 3.4.4).

3.4.1 Working together to an agreed set of values and principles

Given the potential number of local agencies whose activities have an impact on children's play (see Section 1.3.2), opportunities for all children are most likely to be assured if there is close cooperation and an agreed understanding of core values and principles.

The development and implementation of a corporate play policy, providing a framework for all types of indoor and outside play and with outcomes linked to local corporate plans, provides a mechanism for clarifying and agreeing these values and principles. If it is to succeed the policy must be 'owned' and signed up to by all those whose actions have an impact on children's play and must be linked closely with other relevant local strategies and developments, as in Bath and North East Somerset (see Case study 5).

Developing and agreeing key criteria for the development of children's play may require time and negotiation. The central focus must always remain the play needs of

CASE STUDY 5 Bath and North East Somerset (B&NES) play policy

Development of B&NES Play Policy began in March 1999, initiated by the Youth and Community Services Department. A Play Working Party included elected members, officers from education, strategic planning, housing, social services, youth and community, parks, sports and early years sections and representatives from local voluntary sector play and children's organisations. The resulting policy document covers a range of children's play opportunities including staffed adventure playgrounds, non-staffed fixed equipment playgrounds, activity centres, play centres, holiday play schemes and clubs, out-of-school childcare provision, schools and early childhood provision.

An effective corporate play policy is founded on:

- a clear articulation of what is meant by play;
- commitment to respond to children's needs and wishes.

A play policy should be a practical working tool that addresses issues affecting children's play. A play policy will make explicit:

- the objectives of play provision and services;
- the connection between acceptable levels of risk and play;
- a presumption in favour of inclusive provision;
- criteria for a quality play environment;
- play as an aspect of children's cultural life;
- the need to create play opportunities in the general environment.

(PLAYLINK 2002)

children and young people. Children's play policies should have clear links to other strategies and should be an integral element of local Cultural Strategies (DCMS 2000).

Play policies have a role in clarifying the position on risk and safety and supporting a balanced approach to manage the risks so that children's wishes can be met while protecting them from serious harm. In this way the risk of losses from legal action can also be managed (see Section 2.3.3).

In 2002 the Play Safety Forum, a DCMS-sponsored advisory body that brings together the leading national organisations involved in play safety, agreed a position statement on the need to take a balanced approach to safety in play provision (Play Safety Forum 2002). In summary form the statement says: 'Children need and want to take risks when they play. Play provision aims to respond to these needs and wishes by offering children stimulating, challenging environments for exploring and developing their abilities. In doing this, play provision aims to manage the level of risk so that children are not exposed to unacceptable risks of death or serious injury.'

If local agencies are to work together to develop a good range of play opportunities for children and young people there needs to be, in each local authority:

- Development of a play policy and strategy, in partnership with local agencies, as an integral part of the local Cultural Strategy and with outcomes linked to local Corporate Plans, as described in the DCMS-funded document Play as Culture (PLAYLINK 2002).

- A senior officer with explicit responsibility for play development, responsible for and resourced to work across agencies.

- Sufficient resources, in both officer time and money, from each relevant agency, to allow for the strategic development and long-term maintenance of a range of indoor and outdoor, supervised and unsupervised play opportunities.

- A named member of the council and each Local Strategic Partnership who has the brief to champion the play and free-time needs of children and young people across the work of the organisation.

- Commitment from local authority members and senior officers to the strategic and sustained development of children's play opportunities.

We therefore recommend that

Action	Agencies
12 Every local authority works with local partners to develop and promote a corporate play strategy as described in *Play as Culture* (PLAYLINK 2002). (key recommendation)	Local authorities and relevant agencies
13 Where there is currently no play development officer, local authorities, partnerships and other local agencies work with the local play sector to agree a process and timetable for the resourcing, remit and appointment of a post with this responsibility. (key recommendation)	Local authorities, LSPs, other local partnerships and agencies Local play sector
14 Central Government supports the development of local play policies and strategies through strengthening its guidance to local authorities on play in cultural strategies through the active promotion of *Play as Culture* (PLAYLINK 2002) and monitors its impact on the local development of corporate play policies and strategies.	DCMS
15 'Children's Champions' are nominated in each local authority at elected member level and in each LSP.	Local authorities LSPs
16 Local Children and Young People's Strategies (CYPS) address children's play and free-time opportunities.	Lead officers in CYPS partnerships Local play sector
17 The impact on children's play opportunities of the implementation of guidance and monitoring tools promoted by central Government (see Section 1.3.1) is regularly evaluated.	Local authorities, LSPs, DCMS, DTLR, Audit Commission
18 Local authority members and members of LSPs are invited to meet children and young people, visit play provision (both good and poor quality) and learn more about the benefits of play provision.	Local play sector, LSP members, local authority members, EYDCP and local cabinet members

3.4.2 A strategic approach to providing all children with good play opportunities

To ensure the development and maintenance of sustainable play opportunities for all children and young people there needs to be, among those whose actions can affect play opportunities in each locality:

- A systematic play audit.

- Identification of the wishes and needs of specific groups of children and young people of different ages, genders, ethnicity and physical, learning and sensory abilities and in formal childcare.

- Support and training for play providers about the needs of disabled children, black and ethnic minority children and children who might be disadvantaged in their play opportunities.

- An acknowledgement of the different places where children play, including the streets and local open spaces, as well as the different types of supervised and unsupervised play provision possible.

- An understanding of what these different types of play space offer children at different times or in different circumstances.

Establishing what needs to be done

Improving local play opportunities depends, in part, on knowing about local children and their met and unmet needs; what opportunities exist for them now and how well they are used; what support currently exist for play development; what potential exists for developing better play opportunities; and what parents' needs are in relation to their children's free-time activities. This information can be collected through a systematic local play audit which involves children and young people, parents, play providers and those with an interest in public spaces generally (CPC 2002). In some areas, for example Haringey in London, local children and young people have been very involved in local play audits (See Case study 6).

Play audits tend to show gaps in existing provision concerning particular groups of children including those of secondary school age, children from some black and

CASE STUDY 6 Northumberland Park Estate, Haringey – children are the experts

In 2001, 28 children from school years 6 and 9 from the London Borough of Haringey worked with Haringey Play Association to plan the refurbishment of their local outside play space. The children's schools saw the project as important enough to allow them to take part during school hours. The principles underpinning the consultation methods used were discovery, empowerment, democracy and inclusion.

The children, who were seen as the primary experts in play, took part in 'fact-finding' trips, workshops, and model making. The children visited the designated space in the centre of their housing estate where they examined, measured and criticised it. They then constructed a model of the existing space on which they tested different ideas and proposals. The children's plans included facilities for babies and elderly people and environmental improvements, including a community garden, ponds and a quiet area as well as play and youth facilities. They also modelled their ideas for play structures. To ensure the children's expectations were not inhibited by limited experience, they visited and evaluated six different playgrounds.

minority ethnic groups and those who are disabled or have other specific needs (Children's Play Council 2002).

Planning play for all

Meeting the challenge of ensuring play opportunities for all lies firstly in recognising and understanding the diverse but interlinked needs of different groups of children as they grow and develop (see Section 2.3.6). This understanding must then be translated into fully inclusive play provision. Play is one area where difference should be celebrated and in which inclusion and opportunities for all epitomises good practice.

Age

Providing a range of provision for different age groups is crucial. Often it is older children and young people whose needs and wishes need to be met. Some local authorities and partnerships are working closely with older children to identify and provide for their play needs alongside the needs of younger children. For example South Somerset Council (see Case study 7).

Children who are disabled or have specific needs

Including disabled children in play environments is about focusing on diversity and responding to the individual needs and rights of every child. It is about ensuring that each child can join in play activities with other children and that appropriate staff and resources are there to support them. Inclusion benefits everyone. It is about building a community that accepts and values differences and encourages all children, regardless of ability, to play together (Scott 2000).

CASE STUDY 7 South Somerset works in partnership to meet the identified needs of young people

In South Somerset, play provision has focused on the ubiquitous play area suitable for toddlers and young children. However, there were indications that the recreation needs of young people were not being met. So in 1999 the District Council made £80,000 available to support the development of appropriate informal recreation facilities for young people through grant aiding local groups.

Local groups were invited to express an interest in the project and as a result 12 asked to work in partnership with the District Council to develop facilities. The groups included parish councils, village hall committees and recreation trusts. During July 2000 council staff conducted a questionnaire-based survey of young people aged 8–16, surveying primary schools, secondary schools and youth clubs. A total of 1501 questionnaires were returned.

The questionnaire asked young people which facility they would most like to see in their parish and where they would like it to go. Examples were used to demonstrate the types of facilities readily available, and the young people were free to suggest their own ideas. Results showed strong support for multi-use games areas, BMX play tracks, skating areas and youth shelters.

As well as consultation with the young people, there have been open meetings, presentations and newsletter articles to involve the whole community. Where facilities need planning permission, there will also be a statutory consultation process. The District Council is helping the 12 local groups to obtain quotations, identify additional sources of funding and make applications. The proposed facilities consist of 11 BMX play tracks, four multi-use games areas, three kickabout areas (a smaller version of a multi-use games area), five skating areas and three youth shelters. As a result of this project and the interest that it has generated, developing informal recreation facilities for young people is now a key issue in the District Council's Cultural Strategy.

To ensure that play provision is both accessible and attractive to disabled children and young people, service providers need to consider physical access, the ways in which different children communicate with others, suitable transport to and from provision and for trips and outings, how they will let the children and their families know that the provision would welcome them, and what the particular needs of the child are in relation to health and social support (adapted from Scott 2000).

Part III of the Disability Discrimination Act (1995) comes into effect in October 2004, under which play providers will be legally required to have made reasonable adjustments to ensure access to their settings for disabled children and young people. While the actual impact of this legislation is as yet unknown, compliance is likely to be reflected in Best Value and Ofsted criteria (Kidsactive, personal communication).

In playgrounds, low cost solutions and simple changes can make a significant difference to their accessibility for disabled children and young people (CPC and others 2001). Staff training in disability equality/awareness and inclusive play will help in this and in changing practice to make play settings more inclusive.

Supervised play provision has a very important role in promoting and ensuring a wide range of play opportunities for children who might otherwise find it difficult to access unsupervised play opportunities, if they have physical or personal needs which require close adult support (see Case studies 8 and 9).

However, it should be noted that research has shown the extent to which good quality, child-centred free play is by its nature inclusive of disabled children (Maddocks 2001).

CASE STUDY 8 North Hull Adventure Playground is an inclusive play environment

Since its inception the site at the North Hull Adventure Playground has been designed to allow children of all abilities to make full use of the facilities. The whole site is wheelchair accessible and there is specialised equipment including a wheelchair swing and roundabout, a soft play room and a changing room which includes sensory equipment.

The playground provides a short-break care scheme for the children of 25 families in the city of Kingston Upon Hull and surrounding areas in East Riding, Yorkshire. Initially, funding was secured from social services and the local health authority to provide four workers giving one-to-one support to children with additional needs during the school holidays. In 2001, new funding was made available to extend the scheme to after-school club hours and on Saturdays throughout the year.

CASE STUDY 9 The Hip-Hop Scheme in Walthamstow offers an inclusive playscheme

The Hamara Family Project has been established for 12 years and provides a range of services for disabled children and young people. The Project is part of the range of provision supported by Barnardo's London and South East Region. Currently, the project is working with 182 young people aged between 0–19 years and their families. Within the range of services offered by the Hamara Family project, a number of play-based activities are offered. These include: an integrated playscheme during the school holidays as funding allows, the Hip Hop scheme which works to promote the inclusion of disabled children in mainstream out-of-school activities (Hamara Integrated Play and Holiday Opportunities Project) and a holiday club for young people of secondary school age.

Children from black and minority ethnic groups

In Kapasi's research with Asian children and their families, staff at projects that attracted large numbers of Asian children said one of the most important strategies was to create a positive environment in their projects. This meant creating an environment in which Asian children felt comfortable, had a sense of belonging and did not feel excluded or unwelcome (Kapasi 2001).

Staff groups working well as a team was seen as very important by parents of children from black and minority ethnic groups interviewed in a survey in London. Attention to teamwork created an environment where children felt safe and where staff, children and parents were able to enjoy themselves. When there were established staff teams and enthusiastic senior playworkers they tended to involve the local community in the play provision and were more effective in building links with local ethnic communities and in developing parents' trust (Kapasi 2002).

Children in homeless families

There are often particular problems for children in families in temporary accommodation in finding good play opportunities. Lack of space, transience and dislocation are among these. There are, however, some projects trying to support children in homeless families and offer them opportunities to play with other children in similar circumstance or with local children (see Case study 10).

Offering a range of provision

Unsupervised play opportunities

Most children rarely use supervised group childcare or play provision. When not at school they are either at home, playing in the streets near their homes or with friends or relatives (Cole-Hamilton 2002a). As they get older they tend to use parks, playgrounds and other open spaces as places to meet, play and socialise with their friends.

Providing for these needs means adopting polices and practices which make residential streets safer for children's play, locating dedicated play provision in places where children will use it and feel safe, and working with all members of the community to address issues and concerns of adults.

Supervised play provision

Good supervised provision, whether childcare or open access play, tends to be popular with both children and parents. On the whole, children seem to enjoy after-school clubs and in a study of 400 children of 4 to 12 years old, nearly one in five attended the clubs because they enjoyed the opportunity to spend time with friends and the fact that there were more play opportunities than at home (Smith, F 2000). However, a frequent complaint from children is that there are not enough play opportunities and that children's activities are curtailed by lack of choice, space and facilities (Cole-Hamilton 2002a).

Open access facilities, allowing children to come and go as they please, have to provide what local children want or they will not be well used. Supervised play provision is able to offer children a whole range of play experiences and excitement many would otherwise be denied (Head 2001). Supervised play provision includes holiday playschemes, play centres and adventure playgrounds and mobile play provision such as play buses.

CASE STUDY 10 The Finsbury Park Homeless Families Project supported by Islington Play Association

The Finsbury Park project is an example of an outreach play project working with homeless families. Established in 1999 with original funding from the Single Regeneration Budget (SRB) and the local Early Years Development and Childcare Partnership (EYDCP), the project first began work with the under-fives age group, but quickly expanded as it became apparent that the over-fives needed support too. The project, which does not charge the families who use it, offers sessions in specific hostels. In the holidays, the project organises a range of schemes and trips out.

We therefore recommend that

Action	Agencies
19 Play development strategies are routinely grounded in comprehensive local play audits.	Local authority and agencies Local play sector
20 Local officers are given the appropriate support, time and money to undertake local play audits and access audits.	Senior managers and budget holders
21 The provision of inclusive play opportunities becomes the basis for the creation or redevelopment of all children's play provision.	Local authority and agencies Local play sector Senior managers and budget holders
22 Any play audit or analysis of need specifically seeks out and addresses the views of groups of children who make least use of existing opportunities and provision.	Local authority and agencies Local play sector
23 Measures should be taken to improve the availability of places where children can play. Measures should include: ● creating and improving parks and open spaces so they are well lit, overlooked and feel safe; ● providing playgrounds and facilities which are age appropriate, offer challenging play opportunities, in easy-to-get-to, overlooked locations, accessible to disabled children and well maintained; ● providing supervised, open access play provision, staffed by skilled playworkers, which offers a range of both indoor and outside play opportunities and activities; ● improving children's mobility by reducing traffic speed and flow in residential streets and other roads used regularly by children, and considering the introduction of home zones.	Parks, street furniture Parks and play departments Local play and childcare sector Traffic and highways departments
24 Local play planners and providers ensure their provision is inclusive by providing: ● race awareness training; ● inclusive play training for all staff from volunteers to senior managers; ● training in compliance with the Disability Discrimination Act.	EYDCP training and quality assurance Quality Protects Social inclusion trainers

3.4.3 Developing and supporting the local infrastructure

Funding and resources

Secure funding and commitment of resources is fundamental to the provision of good play opportunities for all children and young people. Historically, play provision has suffered from under-funding, short-term funding, and cuts in existing funding. New funding opportunities are often time-limited and frequently targeted towards capital rather then revenue expenditure. If children, families and communities are to benefit from a full range of play provision, secure funding must be available to planners and providers.

Play provision is currently funded from many different sources (see Appendix 4, page 68) and this is likely to continue. Difficulty arises, however, when money is raised in piecemeal fashion with either capital or revenue funding being achieved without the support of the other.

In order for play opportunities to be supported, developed and maintained in a systematic, sustainable manner there needs to be:

- a strategic approach to funding for play at local level;
- funding for the development of policies and strategies as well as for the development of provision;
- funding available which allows for running costs and maintenance as well as the development of new projects;
- funding for the continuation of existing good practice which is proving its worth to children families and communities.

We therefore recommend that

Action	Agencies
25 Those with an interest in play work with budget holders and fundraisers develop sustainable funding for the development and implementation of play policies and strategies. (key recommendation)	Local play sector, relevant local authority budget holders
26 Local government, partnerships and play organisations develop a local framework for funding for children's play which has at its heart the long-term maintenance, development and sustainability of local play opportunities which meet the needs of all children and young people. (key recommendation)	Play sector, local authorities, Local Government Association

Developing and maintaining a skilled workforce

If play provision and childcare are to offer children the range and types of play opportunities they need, the staff must be properly valued, well trained and enthusiastic about their work.

For this to be possible there needs to be:

- Greater recognition, among all those with an interest in and responsibility for children's play, of the difference between the skills and knowledge required for playwork and other types of work with children, emphasising the importance of a firm knowledge base, clearly definable skills and valuing expertise gained through practice.

- An understanding of play and its importance among other staff working with children including, for example, landscape architects, parks and playground managers, teachers, childcare workers and social workers.

- A public discussion about current pay and conditions of work of those involved in playwork and play provision in relation to others working regularly with children and young people.

- A continued emphasis on the development of playwork training and qualifications.

We therefore recommend that

Action	Agencies
27 Work being undertaken by SPRITO on training and qualifications for playwork continue, ensuring that the agreed play values and principles continue to be at its core.	SPRITO, DfES, national and local play sectors
28 Learning and Skills Councils (LSCs) fund and support the development and maintenance of a skilled playwork workforce, working closely with regional play education and training networks.	LSCs, regional play networks
29 Information about the nature, importance and value of playwork be shared and disseminated widely to parents, providers and policy makers at all levels.	National play and playwork sectors
30 Regional development agencies work with regional play training and development organisations to support the development of a skilled, qualified workforce.	RDAs, regional play networks
31 Information and basic training in play and playwork skills is included in the training and education programmes for all staff working with children and young people on a regular basis or managing play provision, supervised or unsupervised.	Play sector, Further and higher education, LSCs, Training Officers in EYDCPs, professional associations
32 The research by the Association of Playworkers (APW) into pay and conditions of service is supported and the results disseminated widely when they are available.	APW, National play and playwork sector, local play sectors
33 Information, advice and training about children's play is offered to people providing formal childcare.	EYDCPs, play services, play associations and networks

Supporting local play networks and associations

Local play associations and networks have an important role in the coordinated development of children's play opportunities. These voluntary sector organisations:

- provide information and advice to local play providers;
- network between play providers;
- provide or lend resources to play providers;
- support the development of play policies and strategies;
- train playworkers;
- provide information and advice to children, parents and others; and
- in some areas operate play provision.

To support the development of play associations in each area there needs to be:

- a wider understanding of the important function these organisations have in the development and support of local play opportunities;
- support from local playworkers and managers in establishing and maintaining local play associations.

We therefore recommend that

Action	Agencies
34 Local agencies investigate what opportunities exist for supporting the development of play associations where they do not exist.	EYDCPs, local authorities, local play sector
35 Existing play associations and networks promote their activities so that agencies in areas where no such networks exist can learn about their value and role.	play associations and networks

3.4.4 Assuring quality

Quality assurance and maintenance of standards is fundamental to the notion of good play opportunities for all. National standards provide a framework for ensuring that play provision, wherever it is, meets the needs of children and young people. The current proposals from the Children and Young People's Unit, that services for children and young people are evaluated in terms of the improvements they make to children's lives (outcomes) is helpful.

There are a number of quality assurance tools currently in use in the play sector as well as the National Daycare Standards, against which Ofsted inspect, and health and safety regulations. Local play providers are increasingly using these tools to monitor and improve the quality of their provision, but there is little systematic analysis of the impact these systems are having on the overall play needs of children and young people.

If nationally agreed standards and quality assurance tools are to contribute to the ongoing development of good play opportunities for all children and young people there needs to be:

- more discussion with children and young people about ways in which quality can be measured in local play provision;
- an evaluation of the use and impact of these tools by local authorities and other play providers.

We therefore recommend that

Action	Agencies
36 The play sector, with local government representatives and national government develop a programme to evaluate the implementation of existing standards in improving local play opportunities and how these impact on children's lives.	Play sector Local government association DCMS, DfES, HSE, DTLR

3.5 The role of central Government

While provision for play must take place at local level, central Government has a vital role to play in promoting and supporting this development through adopting a coordinated strategic approach to the development and maintenance of play for all (Section 3.5.1) that is publicised and backed by senior ministers. Such a strategy should include:

- appropriate direction and guidance to local providers (Section 3.5.2);
- national standards based on outcomes for children (Section 3.5.3);
- adequate strategic resourcing (Section 3.5.4);
- support for the development of a strong infrastructure (Section 3.5.5).

3.5.1 Developing a national strategy for play

All children and young people can only be assured a good range of play opportunities if government shows leadership and direction through the development of a public commitment to children's play. Government departments and agencies need to work closely together to underpin and support the development of local inter-agency working. This will be most effective if:

- Government Ministers and senior officials in all relevant departments develop a greater understanding of the value and importance of play in the lives of children families and communities.
- Government departments whose activities affect children's play opportunities recognise and understand their role and potential impact on children's play (see Section 1.3.2).
- Relevant Government departments work together to develop a strategic approach to development, funding, support and standards for local provision of children's play opportunities within a framework of agreed values, principles and outcomes for children and young people.
- An assessment is made on the impact of new programmes, including the National Childcare Strategy, on the availability of different types of play provision for children, including especially open access, free provision in low income areas.

We therefore recommend that

Action	Agencies
37 Government departments work with the play sector to develop a National Strategy for Play, along the lines of the National Childcare Strategy, grounded in agreed values, principles and desired outcomes for children, which identifies targets for local play provision based on an assessment of the needs and wishes of children and their communities. The Strategy should be linked to the Children and Young People's Unit Strategy and help fulfil its objectives for children's enjoyment. (key recommendation)	DCMS, DfES, DTLR, CYPU, DH, HMT, HO
38 Existing coordination initiatives within Government, involving Department for Culture, Media and Sport, Department for Education and Skills, Children and Young People's Unit, and the Early Years and Childcare Unit, are supported and expanded to include representation from: • the Department for Transport, Local Government and the Regions (sections responsible for local planning, urban policy, housing development, social housing and open spaces); • the Department of Health (Quality Protects Team); and, when appropriate the Home Office (Community Safety Team), Her Majesty's Treasury, the Department for the Environment, Food and Rural Affairs, the Youth Service, the Audit Commission, the Improvement and Development Agency and the Health Development Agency.	DCMS, DfES, other Departments as appropriate

We therefore recommend that (continued)

Action	Agencies
39 This cross-cutting group work closely with public and voluntary sector agencies to: ● agree and promote the values and principles underpinning the Government's approach to children's play throughout their relevant work programmes; ● develop objectives and detailed strategic plans aimed at providing the guidance, support and resources required to support local provision of good play opportunities for school-aged children and young people; ● discuss ways in which it can support the development of a long-term funding strategy for children's play; ● agree a programme of research into the impact of the National Childcare Strategy and other relevant programmes on children's play provision.	DCMS, DfES, CYPU, play sector

3.5.2 Direction and guidance to local providers

The Government needs to promote universal access to publicly funded services and initiatives through direction and guidance to local planners and providers of services to children and young people. For this to be effective for children's play, guidance needs to:

- give information and direction about ways in which the whole range of children's play needs can be met;
- advise on the amount of space required for ensuring good play opportunities in different types of area with differing populations;
- be sufficiently flexible to meet local needs while still ensuring provision for all;
- be based on agreed outcomes for children, achieved by ensuring access to a range of play opportunities;
- monitor and support the implementation of the Disability Discrimination Act 1995 in children's play provision, as agreed by DTLR.

Monitoring the implementation of existing guidance and strengthening it in the light of its effects on children's play opportunities is also important if children, families and communities are to gain the maximum benefit.

We therefore recommend that

Action	Agencies
40 Government and the play sector work closely together to develop outcome indicators as targets for the local development of play opportunities.	DCMS, DTLR, DfES, DH, CYPU, play sector
41 Government departments and agencies review existing guidance and practice development documents with a view to assessing the impact they might have on children's play opportunities.	DCMS, DTLR, DfES, HO, DH, AC
42 The play sector work with relevant government departments to develop a programme of monitoring and evaluating the effects of guidance on children's play opportunities.	Play sector, DCMS, DTLR, DfES, HO, DH, AC
43 The implementation of the DDA in children's play and play provision is monitored.	DRC
44 A Code of Practice for full implementation of the DDA in children's outdoor play space is developed, as agreed by DTLR.	DTLR

3.5.3 National standards based on outcomes for children

If nationally agreed standards and quality assurance tools are to contribute to the ongoing development of good quality play opportunities for all children and young people, there needs to be:

- an evaluation of the impact of the National Daycare Standards and quantitative and qualitative spatial standards such as the Six-Acre Standard (NPFA 2001) on children's play opportunities in formal childcare and play provision;

- a discussion about ways in which outcome measures can be developed, based on the seven play objectives defined in the play sector document *Best Play* (NPFA 2000);

- a thorough evaluation of other quality assurance tools including, for example, *Aiming High* (KCN 1996), *Quality in Play* (Conway and Farley 2001), *The First Claim* (Play Wales 2001) and schemes currently being developed, once they have been well used within the sector.

We therefore recommend that

Action	Agencies
45 There is systematic monitoring of the implementation of National Daycare Standards in out-of-school childcare and play provision and their impact on children's play.	DfES, Ofsted
46 There is monitoring of the impact of the expansion of childcare provision on the availability of free, open access play provision, especially in areas with high numbers of low income families.	DfES
47 Development work is undertaken on the use of outcome measures based on the seven play objectives defined in the play sector document *Best Play*.	Play sector, DCMS, DfES, DTLR
48 A thorough evaluation is undertaken of quality assurance tools including, for example, *Aiming High, Quality in Play* and *The First Claim* and schemes currently being developed, once they have become better established.	DfES
49 Research is undertaken to develop comprehensive spatial standards for children's outdoor play that are sufficiently flexible to meet local needs while still ensuring adequate space for children and young people's play and free-time activities.	DTLR, play sector

3.5.4 Adequate strategic resourcing

Although there is funding for play available through a range of government funding programmes including the New Opportunities Fund, the Children's Fund and Neighbourhood Renewal Funds (see Section 2.3.10) this money is usually short-term, linked to new initiatives and frequently for capital expenditure.

According to one educated 'guesstimate', based on extrapolation from work undertaken in a London Borough, the cost of bringing England's play areas up to standard would be around £500 million. This would include: replacement of equipment considered beyond useable life or no longer compliant with latest standards; some resiting and rationalisation (away from busy roads and immediately overlooked by tower blocks); piecemeal play area development in parks and installing dog-proof fencing and self-closing gates (Anderson, personal communication to CPC).

If children's play opportunities are to be sustained, there must be a commitment to long-term, revenue funding as well as capital and 'start-up' money. The potential for children's play opportunities to become income-generating is low, especially in the economically deprived areas where they are most needed.

We therefore recommend that

Action	Agencies
50 **There is an urgent and comprehensive review of national funding for children's play with a view to developing a long-term commitment and strategy for on-going funding for local authorities and agencies to develop and maintain local opportunities for children's play which ensure agreed outcomes for children. (key recommendation)**	DCMS, play sector, HMT, DTLR, DfES, DH, LGA
51 Detailed research is undertaken into the potential costs of providing good play opportunities for all children and young people.	DCMS, HMT, local authorities and agencies

3.5.5 Support for the development of a strong infrastructure

Local provision for children's play needs to be supported by the development of a skilled, motivated, valued workforce; national agencies which support and undertake research, monitoring and policy development and information management and dissemination.

This report has highlighted existing areas of academic research, especially about the benefits of play to children's healthy development. However, it is clear that there needs to be more systematic research into, for example:

- the value of different types of play provision to different children at different times and in different circumstances;
- the long-term value of play in children's development, based on longitudinal studies;
- 'what works' in children's play.

We therefore recommend that

Action	Agencies
52 **Government works with the play sector to support a national agency or unit within Government to guide and develop the play sector in practice development, research, evaluation, policy development and information dissemination with a brief to include all types of play opportunities for children and young people. (key recommendation)**	DCMS, DfES, DTLR, DH, play sector
53 Government works with the play sector and higher education sector to continue to research the evidence base and 'what works' in the provision of play opportunities.	DCMS, universities and colleges of higher education

Action	Agencies
54 Government continues to fund and work closely with workforce development agencies such as SPRITO in the development and maintenance of training and qualifications for playworkers.	DfES, SPRITO, further and higher education
55 Government develops its support for play research and policy development in partnership with the Children's Play Policy Forum, the Children's Play Council and other agencies.	DCMS, CPC, CPPF
56 Government develops its support for the Children's Play Information Service.	DCMS, CPIS

Conclusions

In this report the Children's Play Council makes the case for public funding and strategic planning for the development, support and maintenance of good play opportunities for children and young people in England.

However, this can only be achieved through close cooperation among all those with an interest in and whose actions impact on children's play. This means children and young people, parents, community groups, playworkers and managers, local authorities and other agencies, regional agencies, playwork educators and trainers, voluntary sector play organisations and government departments all working together with a common objective: to ensure that all children and young people in England have the opportunities they want and need for play.

The Children's Play Council would like to thank the Department for Culture, Media and Sport for giving us the opportunity to undertake this work.

Appendix 1:
Key underpinning documents

The New Charter for Children's Play

The Charter for Children's Play was first published in 1992, and was the result of a collaborative exercise involving agencies with an interest in promoting and sustaining quality play opportunities for all children. The Charter was revised in 1998 and forms one of the underpinning documents for the development of children's play.

The New Charter for Children's Play asserts that:

- All children need to play and have a right to play. Children of all ages should be able to play freely and confidently on their own and with other children.

- Parents and other carers should respect and value their children's play and try to maximise their opportunities for safe and stimulating play within and outside the home.

- All children should have equal access to play opportunities and services.

- All children should be able to play safely out of doors wherever they live, in towns, cities and in the countryside. Older children should also be able to get around safely on their own.

- Central and local government and voluntary organisations should think creatively and strategically about children and their play needs.

- All children should have access to a range of good quality early years play and out-of-school services such as play centres, holiday playschemes, adventure playgrounds, after-school clubs, playgroups, toy libraries and play buses.

- All schools should support and facilitate children's play. Play and learning are not separate; play is part of learning and learning is part of play. Learning through play supports and enriches learning through formal education.

- Play opportunities should challenge and stimulate children's abilities but not threaten their survival or well-being.

- Hospital admissions, visits to a doctor, or a stay in temporary accommodation are some of the situations where children are in strange surroundings, perhaps experiencing fear, pain, anxiety and discomfort. They should be provided with play opportunities led by staff and volunteers who understand their special needs.

- All playwork education and training should be flexible, adaptable, reflective of existing good practice in play and should involve a significant fieldwork practice component.

(Children's Play Council 1998)

National Occupational Standards: values and principles

In order to inform and underpin the provision of consistent play opportunities for children and young people, play-workers have developed a set of values and principles about children and play which are set out in the National Strategy for Playwork and Training. These are that:

- Children's views must be taken into account.

- It is the responsibility of the community to ensure that all children have access to rich, stimulating environments that are free from unacceptable risk, which allow children to explore through freely chosen play.

- Children's freedom to play must be preserved.

- That all children, irrespective of gender, background, cultural or racial origin, or individual ability, should have equal access to good play opportunities.

- Children should feel confident that the adults involved in play welcome and value them as individuals.

- The child's control of their own activity is a crucial factor in enriching their experience and adults need to recognise and support this.

- There should be no task or product required of the play by those not engaged in it.

- An appropriate level of risk is fundamental to play, allowing children to develop confidence and abilities and it is the responsibility of play providers to respond with 'exciting and stimulating environments that balance risks appropriately'.

- Adult encouragement and responsiveness must be available when needed and appropriate.

(see NPFA and others 2000)

These values and principles are currently under review but are unlikely to change dramatically.

Best Play: objectives for play provision

In 2000 play professionals also developed a set of child-centred objectives for play provisions. These offer a set of outcomes to help clarify the role play provision should have in the lives and development of children and young people.

The seven objectives of play provision are:

Objective 1: The provision extends the choice and control that children have over their play, the freedom they enjoy and the satisfaction they gain from it.

Objective 2: The provision recognises the child's need to test boundaries and responds positively to that need.

Objective 3: The provision manages the balance between the need to offer risk and the need to keep children safe from harm.

Objective 4: The provision maximises the range of play opportunities.

Objective 5: The provision fosters independence and self-esteem.

Objective 6: The provision fosters children's respect for others and offers opportunities for social interaction.

Objective 7: The provision fosters the child's well-being, healthy growth and development, knowledge and understanding, creativity and capacity to learn.

(NPFA and others 2000)

Appendix 2:
Play theories and philosophies

At the end of the nineteenth and beginning of the twentieth centuries, observation of play in the young of various species gave rise to a number of ideas about how play might confer survival benefits, strengthening the body, rehearsing adult roles, developing adult skills, releasing potentially destructive 'excess' energy. The prolonged childhood of the human young was seen as necessary to develop the more complex skills and capacities required to become effective as an adult human (NPFA and others 2000).

More recently, writers have recognised two basic viewpoints towards the importance of play – one that says it is a 'preparation for the future' and the other, that it is an 'adjustment to the present' (Sutton-Smith, in Goldstein 1994). Others have identified play as reflecting different developmental stages which children pass through. In much of the literature, the idea of play evolving into gradually more sophisticated forms as the child matures is evident (Street 2002).

According to Bruce (1997), historically play was originally seen as a break from work; another early theory saw it as the way that children 'let off steam from the pressure that work builds up inside them'. Gradually however, from the 1920s onwards, interest in childhood play grew and it became increasingly seen as helping children to learn. Sigmund Freud's work was a significant influence highlighting the emotional aspects of childhood play, with play being recognised as one way in which children could learn to control their feelings and to deal with anxieties and conflicts (in Street 2002).

Bruce notes that 'as it was gradually realised that emotional and social development are helped by play, those interested in young children began to understand that play also helps children to think'. Piaget's theories of how children take in and make sense of experiences, took

the understanding of children's play a stage further in the 1940s, with much greater attention then shifting to the importance of play in encouraging cognitive development (in Street 2002).

By the late 1980s, Rogers and Sawyers' analysis of the importance of play in children's lives (1988) suggests that play is an important element of children's motivation and therefore participation in society. They suggest that children cannot be passive recipients of play and since they are actively involved, this encourages autonomous thinking. They also suggest that play provides the opportunities to develop the skills of actively building environments; gives children the chance to make sense of things that have been done to them by turning them into activities they can control and understand (in Street 2002).

Rogers and Sawyers go on to suggest that play helps cognitive development in a number of ways. It is an active form of learning that unites the mind, body and spirit; provides the opportunity to practice new skills and functions; allows children to consolidate previous learning; allows them to retain their playful attitudes, a learning set which contributes to flexibility in problem-solving; develops creative and aesthetic appreciation; enables children to learn about learning – through curiosity, invention, persistence; reduces the pressure or tension that otherwise is associated with having to achieve or needing to learn; and provides a minimum of risks and penalties for mistakes.

From the literature on play, Rogers and Sawyers also identify four other areas where play is important: in encouraging children to develop problem-solving skills; in supporting their language development and literacy, in developing their social skills; and in expressing their emotions.

More recently play theorists have been considering play's potential role in human development and evolution. Alluded to at the turn of the twentieth century in Hall's Recapitulation Theory (1904), and supported and developed in the 1970s, play now features as an important consideration in the current rapid development of the brain sciences and the flood of neurobiological data (Hughes 1996). Citing Huttenlocher's work on brain imaging technology, Sutton-Smith (1997) states that in the first ten years of life, human children have at least twice the synaptic capacity as children over ten, while others link this 'plasticity' to the effects of 'enriched' environments. This increasing understanding of the working of the brain is also leading to a reassessment of what is now called emotional intelligence. It is also giving rise to suggestions that play in young children may have a critical role in the enlargement of brain capacity (NPFA and others 2000).

In his most recent book, Hughes suggests that increasingly, play is believed to be the outcome of a vital biological drive, in much the same way as eating and sexual activity are recognised as the results of other biological drives. He goes on to suggest that this play drive may exist to guarantee that, as vulnerable and naive young organisms, children can engage with the world they live in, in a way which suits their abilities but which is also highly efficient. This, he argues, is essential for continued survival and development. The play drive is important because it has a vital role in the development of the human ability to adapt to changing environmental conditions (Hughes 2001).

Although theories about the significance of play to children and in their development abound, researchers and theorists agree that the role of play in child development is underexplored. Nevertheless, the theories and findings do allow some reasonably firm conclusions to be drawn about the contribution play makes to learning, health and well-being (Street 2002).

Appendix 3:
National and local initiatives which impact on children's play

1 Central Government initiatives

Department for Culture, Media and Sport
Financial support for SPRITO, Children's Play Council, Children's Play Information Service, Children's Play Policy Forum
Recognition of Play Safety Forum
Review of NOF funding
Cultural Strategies Guidance

Children and Young People' Unit
Children and Young People's Strategy
CYPU's core principles on consulting children
Children's Fund

Department of Health
Quality Protects
Valuing People: a new strategy for learning disability for the twenty-first century

Department for Transport, Local Government and the Regions
Home Zone Challenge
Planning Policy Guidance notes: PPG 17 and PPG3
Urban Green Spaces Task Force
Beacon Councils
Strong local leadership – quality public services
Road Safety Initiatives

Department for Education and Skills
Ofsted Daycare Standards
National Childcare Strategy
Review of Playwork Education and Training Strategy
Connexions
Financial support for SPRITO, Kidsactive and PLAYLINK projects
Extended Schools

Audit Commission
Best Value Performance Indicators for play
Quality of Life Indicators

Other
Qualifications and Curriculum Authority (QCA) framework
Youth Justice Board summer schemes
Inland Revenue (Tax Credits)
Community Safety Initiatives
Cross-cutting reviews of public space, children at risk and childcare

2 Local government and partnerships

Community Strategies
Local Strategic Partnerships
Community Safety Strategies
Children and Young People Strategic Partnership
Children's Plans
Health Action Zones
Early Years Development and Childcare Partnerships
Neighbourhood Regeneration
Home Zones
Best Value
Green Flag Award Scheme for parks

3 Play sector initiatives

Association of Play Workers
Raise playwork profile
Unionisation of play work
Research into pay and conditions

Equipe: (EU) £1.9 million
Social Enterprise, training, playwork: skills

Kidsactive
P.I.P.: Playwork Inclusion Project (funded by DfES)

London Play
Evaluation of *Quality in Play* QA scheme
Applying for WFTC accreditation
Play Strategy for London

PLAYLINK
Free play network (3 years)
Open Access Registration Support (OARS) (DfES)

SPRITO: Playwork Unit
Regional: Foundations for the Future
Quality Framework:
 – endorsements at local and regional level
 – programmes
 – code of practice
 – register of trainers
 – approving material
NOS
 – Communications
 – Review and devise NOS

(CPC January 2002, Play Policy Seminar)

Appendix 4:
Funding programmes and initiatives being accessed for play provision

Early Excellence Centres

Childcare Strategy – Training and Professional Development

Children's Fund

NOF Better Play

Other NOF programmes

DCMS Funding of CPC, CPPF

Neighbourhood Renewal and Regeneration Programme

Local Regeneration

'Section 106' – planning gain

Groundwork Trust

Sure Start

Home Office – Family Support

Home Office – Active Communities

Qualify Protects sub-objective 6.3 for inclusive play provision

European Social Fund and other European Initiatives

(CPC January 2002, Play Policy Seminar)

References

Adams, E and Ingham, S (1998) *Changing Places – Children's participation in environmental planning.*
The Children's Society

Armitage, A (1999) *What do you mean you don't like it? Interpreting children's perceptions of the playground as an aid to designing effective playspace*, paper for International Toy Research Conference, Halmstad, Sweden

Attfield, I (2001) *'Me too!' A report by Mencap on play, leisure and childcare for children and young people with a disability in the Metropolitan Borough of Dudley.* Mencap

Bruce, T (1997) *Helping Young Children to Play.* Hodder & Stoughton

Bruce, T (2001) *Learning Through Play: Babies, toddlers and the foundation years.* Hodder & Stoughton

Bishop, J and Curtis, M *eds* (2001) *Play Today in the Primary School Playground.* Open University Press

Candappa, M (2000) *Extraordinary Childhoods: The social lives of refugee children.* Thomas Coram Research Unit, University of London

Carvel, J (1999) Play is out, early learning is in. *The Guardian* 23 June, p.5

Children's Play Council (1998) *The New Charter for Children's Play.* The Children's Society

Children's Play Council (2002) *More than Swings and Roundabouts: Planning for outdoor play.*
National Children's Bureau

Children's Play Council, Kidsactive and Mencap (2001) *Parliamentary Briefing: Children with Disabilities* (Play Areas Bill), Mencap

Cole-Hamilton, I 'Something good and fun: children and parents' views on play and out-of-school provision' *in* Cole-Hamilton, I, Harrop, A and Street, C (2002a) *Making the Case for Play: Gathering the evidence.*
National Children's Bureau

Cole-Hamilton, I 'The State of Play: a survey of play professionals in England' *in* Cole-Hamilton, I, Harrop, A and Street, C (2002b) *Making the Case for Play: Gathering the evidence.* National Children's Bureau

Cole-Hamilton, I, Harrop, A and Street, C (2002) *Making the Case for Play: Gathering the evidence.*
National Children's Bureau

Conway, M and Farley, T (2001) *Quality in Play: Quality assurance for children's play providers.* London Play

CYPU (2001a) *Building a Strategy for Children and Young People: Consultation document.* Children and Young People's Unit, Department for Education and Skills

CYPU (2001b) *Learning to Listen: Core principles for the involvement of children and young people.*
Children and Young People's Unit, Department for Education and Skills, London

Davis, A and Jones, L (1997) Whose neighbourhood? Whose quality of life? Developing a new agenda for children's health in urban settings, *Health Education Journal*, 56, pp.350–63

DCMS (2000) *Creating Opportunities: Guidance for local authorities in England on Local Cultural Strategies.* Department for Culture, Media and Sport

DfEE (2001) *Promoting Play in Out-of-School Childcare.* Department for Education and Employment (now Department for Education and Skills)

DTLR (2002) *Strong Local Leadership – Quality Public Services.* Department for Transport, Local Government and the Regions

Dietz, W (2001) The obesity epidemic in young children, *British Medical Journal*, 322, 7282, pp.313–14

Greenhalgh, L and Worpole, K (1995) *Park Life: Urban parks and social renewal.* A Report by Comedia in association with Demos, Comedia

Guddemi, M and Jambor, T (1992) A Right to Play Texas, *Proceedings of the American Affiliate of the International Association for the Child's Right to Play,* September 17–20

Harrop, A 'The planning and location of play provision in England: a mapping exercise' *in* Cole-Hamilton, I, Harrop, A and Street, C (2002) *Making the Case for Play: Gathering the evidence.* National Children's Bureau

Head, T (2001) *Making Sense: Playwork in practice.* PLAYLINK

Hood, S (2001) *The State of London's Children Report.* Office of the Children's Rights Commissioner for London

Hughes, B (1996) *Play Environments: A Question of Quality.* PLAYLINK

Hughes, B (2001) *Evolutionary Playwork and Reflective Analytic Practice.* Routledge

Hughes, L (1998) *My Dream Site: Research with traveller children around the issue of sites.* The Children's Society

Kapasi, H (2001) *Asian Children Play: Increasing access to play provision for Asian children,* second edition. PlayTrain

Kapasi, H (2002) *Playing in Parallel: A study of access to play provision by Black and minority children in London.* London Play

KCN (1996) *Aiming High: Kids' Clubs Network Quality Assurance Scheme for out of school clubs.* Kids' Clubs Network

KCN (2001) *Looking to the Future for Children and Family: A Report of the Millennium Childcare Commission.* Kids' Clubs Network

Macintyre, C (2001) *Enhancing Learning through Play.* David Fulton

Maddocks, J (2001) *Report from research on the Kidsactive approach to play work.* Kidsactive, unpublished

Matthews, H and Limb, M (2000) *Exploring the 'Fourth Environment': Young people's use of place and their views on their environment.* Centre for Children and Youth, University College, Northampton

McKendrick, J (2000) *The Dangers of Safe Play.* School of Social Sciences, Glasgow Caledonian University

McKendrick, J, Bradford, M and Fielder, A (2000a) Kid Customer? Commercialization of playspace and the commodification of childhood, *Childhood,* 7, 3, pp.295–314

McKendrick, J, Fielder, A and Bradford, M (2000b) Enabling play or sustaining exclusion? Commercial playgrounds and disabled children, *The North West Geographer,* 3, pp.32–49

Mental Health Foundation (1999) *Bright Futures: Promoting children and young people's mental health.* Mental Health Foundation

Moorcock, K (1998) *Swings and Roundabouts: The danger of safety in outside play environments.* Sheffield Hallam University Press

Moss, P (2000) From Children's Services to Children's Spaces, *NCVCCO Annual Review Journal*, 2, pp.19–35

National Playing Fields Association, Children's Play Council and PLAYLINK (2000) *Best Play: What play provision should do for children.* National Playing Fields Association (available from Children's Play Council)

NPFA (2001) *The Six Acre Standard: Minimum standards for outdoor playing space.* National Playing Fields Association

New Economics Foundation (2001) *Prove It! Measuring Impacts of Renewal: Findings and recommendations.* Groundwork UK

O'Brien, M, Rustin, M and Greenfield, J (2000) *Childhood Urban Space and Citizenship: Child-sensitive urban regeneration.* University of North London

Petrie, P, Storey, P and Candappa M (2000a) *Inclusive Play, Towards a framework for improved practice.* Thomas Coram Research Unit, Institute of Education, University of London

Petrie, P, Egharevba, I, Oliver, C and Poland, G (2000b) *Out of School Lives, Out of School Services.* The Stationery Office

PLAYLINK (2002) *Play as Culture: Incorporating play in Cultural Strategies.* PLAYLINK

Play Safety Forum (2002) *Managing Risks in Play Provision: A position statement.* Children's Play Council

Play Wales (2000) *The State of Play 2000.* Play Wales

Play Wales (2001) *The First Claim: A framework for playwork quality assessment.* Play Wales

Rogers, C and Sawyers, J (1988) *Play in the Lives of Children.* National Association for the Education of Young Children, Washington

Scottish Executive (2001) *For Scotland's Children – Better integrated services: An action plan,* Scottish Executive

Scott, R (2000) *Side by Side: Guidelines for inclusive play.* Kidsactive

Smith, F (2000) *Child-Centred After School and Holiday Childcare.* Department of Geography, Brunel University, Uxbridge

Smith, S 'Children at play' Mills, J and Mills R eds (2000) *Childhood Studies: A reader in perspectives of childhood.* Routledge

Stobart, T (1992) *Children Today in Devon: Playing in the countryside – a study of rural children's services.* National Children's Play and Recreation Unit

Street, C 'The value of children's play and play provision: a systematic review of the literature' *in* Cole-Hamilton, I, Harrop, A and Street, C (2002) *Making the Case for Play: Gathering the evidence*. National Children's Bureau

Sutton-Smith, B 'Does Play Prepare the Future?' *in* Goldstein, J ed. (1994) *Toys, Play and Child Development*. Cambridge University Press

Sutton-Smith, B (1997) *The Ambiguity of Play*. Harvard, University Press, Cambridge, Mass

Valentine, G (1997) A safe place to grow up? Parenting, perceptions of children's safety and the rural idyll, *Journal of Rural Studies*, 13, 2, pp.137–48

Valentine, G and Holloway, S (1999) *Cyberkids: Children's social networks, 'virtual communities' and on line spaces*. Department of Geography University of Sheffield

Watson, N, Barnes, B, Corker, M, Cunningham-Burley, S, Davis, J, Priestley, M, Shakespeare, T (2000) *Life as a Disabled Child: A qualitative study of young people's experiences and perspectives*. Department of Nursing Studies, University of Edinburgh

Wheway, R and Millward, A (1997) *Child's Play: Facilitating play on housing estates*. Chartered Institute of Housing

Woolley, H, Dunn, J, Spencer, C, Short, T and Rowley, G (1999) Children describe their experiences of the city centre: a qualitative study of the fears and concerns which may limit their full participation, *Landscape Research*, 24, 3, pp.287–310